The Politics
of Doomsday

The Politics of Doomsday

FUNDAMENTALISTS OF THE FAR RIGHT

ERLING JORSTAD

abingdon press • nashville & new york

THE POLITICS OF DOOMSDAY

Copyright © 1970 by Abingdon Press

ISBN 0-687-31730-4

Library of Congress Catalog Card Number: 70-112332

SET UP, PRINTED AND BOUND BY THE
PARTHENON PRESS, AT NASHVILLE,
TENNESSEE, UNITED STATES OF AMERICA

To Helen

Acknowledgments

I have become indebted to many persons in the preparation of this book. None should be held in any way responsible for any errors in fact or judgment; those are mine. I gratefully thank Professors Howard Bavender, Peter Beckman, David L. Brye, Henry B. Clark, Robert T. Handy, James Johnson, Arnold F. Krugler, Olaf Millert, Alan Nelson, Ernest R. Sandeen, and Joseph Shaw. Special thanks must be made to Professor William F. McKee for services rendered far beyond the call of friendship. I have been helped also by two students, Darrel Jodock and Richard Koch. As those who have used the St. Olaf College Library know, their tasks are lightened considerably by the splendid cooperation of the library staff. I am especially indebted to Miss Charlotte Jacobson for procuring materials with humor and dispatch, and to Forrest Brown and Homer Mason for their help with my many requests. My debt to my wife can be suggested but never adequately expressed by the dedication of this book.

Foreword

Throughout American history the nation's religious groups and the federal government have carefully preserved the wall of separation raised up by the First Amendment between church and state. In contrast to many of their European counterparts, American ecclesiastical and civil leaders have been able to find workable solutions to such vexatious problems as parochial education, taxing church property, oaths of allegiance and the licensing of clergymen. Few observers would challenge the conclusion so ably presented by Sidney Mead that until recent times the United States had successfully formed a society founded on clear religious principles without the encumbrance of an established church.[1]

The events of the 1960's, however, disclosed that the churches were caught up in a profound transformation. Old forms yielded to new and the consensus of the past 180 years was no longer adequate to the demands of a new era. For the first time Americans faced problems such as the renovated posi-

[1] Sidney E. Mead, *The Lively Experiment: The Shaping of Christianity in America* (New York: Harper & Row, 1963).

tion of the Roman Catholic Church following the election of a Catholic president and the reforms of Vatican II. They had to adjust to the Supreme Court rulings on Bible reading and prayer in public schools. The Great Society they so strongly endorsed in 1964 broke new ground by offering public funds to parochial schools. It employed ecclesiastical officials in the administration of the antipoverty program, and it granted federal loans to church-related colleges. The wall of the First Amendment still stood intact, but it had been given a thorough renovation.

The churches themselves found new resources to strengthen their ministry to the nation. The ecumenical movement, in its many dimensions, stood out as the most prominent of all experiments. Scholars of Catholic, Jewish, and Protestant loyalties worked together in biblical and theological research. Old denominational animosities melted in the enthusiasm for a united witness. Clergymen and laity found in civil rights a common cause which exacted every ounce of dedication they could enlist. Most religious groups showed an eagerness for experimentation, be it in architecture, in liturgical reform, in parish education programs, or in extensive use of the mass media. To be sure, each innovation met with resistance and sharp criticism at one point or another. But the momentum for change—the all-purpose command was "relevance"—clearly dominated the religious scene in the 1960's. For better or worse, the churches and synagogues would not return to the stability of earlier times.

Throughout the era, a tiny but vehement band of Protestants denounced every change as being for the worse, and not only "worse" but in fact disastrous for the cause of Christianity in the world. Instead of relevance their leaders called for a "Twentieth Century Reformation," a "Christian Crusade," a total sweeping out of every element in American church life which deviated from their understanding of pure New Testament Christianity. American church people stood not on the threshold of a creative new age, but on the brink of total destruction. The myriad of changes was absolute proof that this nation and the world now faced the Last Days. Satan had cleverly disguised his soldiers as clergymen who had convinced most Americans they were simply trying to make Christianity meaningful in society. What this really meant was that Satan had laid his plans for the

12

Battle of Armageddon. Soon, at any moment now, he would come out of hiding and challenge God for control of this planet. Unless America repented at once, it would face the horrors of doomsday.

These leaders were "the fundamentalists of the far right," or "ultrafundamentalists." [2] Their bill of particulars was very long and precise. The changes in church-state relations, the ecumenical movements, and the increasing social outreach of the churches were nothing more than the Devil fornicating with the Whore of Babylon (Rev. 17). An insidious conspiracy was at work uniting Washington, Rome, Moscow, and Geneva (the World Council of Churches) into the kingdom of Lucifer. Every social reform, from civil rights to fluoridation, from the income tax to social security, was the creation of the Communists who took orders from Satan.

America simply did not realize how perilous its condition had become. The Devil's agents were everywhere; in the television and radio networks, at Wheaton College, in the Billy Graham ministry, in most seminaries, schools, and at every level of government. These agents were not actually Communists themselves; no, they were too clever for that. They were the liberals and the moderates and the conservatives in government, church life, education, and indeed every major occupation who were "pro-Communist" because they were not wholeheartedly supporting the only true Christians left on this planet. America, repent!

Prophets of doom have usually appeared during times of crisis in American history, and those of the 1960's were not completely unique. What is distinctive about their program is primarily the subject of this book. I am aware the subject matter is highly controversial. It deals with the very recent past and focuses on deeply felt religious and political convictions. Neither of these subjects lends itself to unemotional analysis. Thus, it may be useful here to outline the structure of this study and to summarize briefly the conclusions.

In the first half of the book I trace the rise of this movement from the late nineteenth century to its position of prominence in the mid-1960's. Fundamentalism of the far right was

[2] My definitions of these and other terms such as "far" and "radical right" will be presented in the text, especially chaps. 6 and 7.

created by the merging of the ultrafundamentalist theology, which first appeared in the 1930's, and the political ideology of the far right, which was created in the late 1950's. These two currents were blended into a single stream by the leaders of ultrafundamentalism at about the time Senator John F. Kennedy announced his candidacy for the presidency of the United States.

This was not a coincidence. The election campaign, the style, and the policies of the New Frontiersmen, especially concerning Cuba and civil rights convinced the potential fundamentalist of the far right that he must join in the strongest possible protest to halt the rush of his beloved nation into the hands of Satan via communism. As they denounced the president, Congress, and the government in general, the leaders of ultrafundamentalism discovered a rapid increase in both receipts and national attention concerning their programs. They also discovered their ideas and goals harmonized very closely with those groups of the political far right, exemplified by the John Birch Society. The many radical right groups found a common cause in working side by side during the presidential campaign of 1964. By the end of that year, ultrafundamentalism, which at one time carefully limited itself to ecclesiastical matters, had established a national reputation for itself as an integral contributor to the entire far right crusade.

I have ended the first half with the immediate repercussions of the 1964 presidential election. By then its leaders had achieved their long-desired goal of directing well-financed, well-publicized action programs. Their collective annual budget ran into the millions of dollars. By their standards they had started the "Twentieth Century Reformation," the "Christian Crusade." [3]

Some significant changes in this movement have occurred between that time and the present. Dr. Carl McIntire, the prime mover, has run into serious criticism of his leadership from several close associates; the Supreme Court has upheld the Fairness Doctrine concerning radio broadcasting. Most far rightists, including the ultrafundamentalists, have found in Governor George Wallace the messiah they thought they had lost after the 1964 presidential election. However, important as these are, by stopping the nar-

[3] I have used some source materials of the ultrafundamentalists published after my own cutoff point. These were used because they more accurately expressed certain points of view already established before 1965.

14

rative at 1964 we gain perspective for a more balanced assessment and avoid the difficulties of trying to keep up with every day's new events within a movement which has not ended.

Furthermore, the historical narrative yields only a partial answer to the questions of the appeal and influence of ultrafundamentalism in American church life. In the last half I discuss doctrine, ideology, and action programs. I suggest potential followers find the movement highly appealing because it furnishes them with the assurance that they are the only Christians in America and only their program can save this nation from self-destruction. This assurance is based on the remarkably cohesive blend of theology, political ideology, and directed activities offered to them by their leaders. I explore at length the processes by which the believers translated these doctrines into action. By this kind of exploration we can reach a more complete understanding of the ultrafundamentalists' conviction that they alone speak for God.

This study does not include the kinds of insight that the fields of psychology and sociology could furnish concerning the motives of the participants for their convictions and behavior. As helpful as this information is for a complete understanding, I have found several obstacles to its inclusion in this book. To the best of my knowledge only a handful of empirical studies on this subject have been completed. These are works of solid scholarship, but the authors themselves chose to limit their samplings to case studies, and the results, by their own estimation, cannot be considered complete enough to serve as documentation for the entire radical right. Further, no comparable study as such has been conducted among the followers of the American and International Councils of Christian Churches and the Christian Crusade, the primary agencies for ultafundamentalism. Another obstacle has been the great difficulty of students of the movement in receiving permission from its leaders for field-survey, research studies among the supports. Apparently they are deeply suspicious of all scholars outside their tradition, especially those interested in conducting behavioral investigations into their enterprises.[4]

[4] See, for example, the account of the difficulties experienced by Prof. Sheilah R. Koeppen when trying to interview supporters of Dr. Fred C. Schwarz: Koeppen, "Dissensus and Discontent: The Clientele of the Christian Anti-Communism Crusade," (Ph.D. diss., Stanford University, 1967), pp. 16-22; Ira S.

I hope that in some future time some student of the far right might have the opportunity to conduct field surveys. In light of the obstacles encountered, then, I have followed the suggestion of Hans Toch that "although we cannot deduce the motives of individual members from ideology, we can use ideology to construct an image of the *ideal* member—a hypothetical person who would feel uniquely at home in the movement." [5]

Some groundwork in this field has already been published. Two extensive bibliographies of this research are: "Freedom Institute Bibliography" (1969), published by Iowa Wesleyan College, Mt. Pleasant, Iowa; and the January, February, and April, 1969, issues of a newsletter, *The Dixon Line,* Box 278, Los Alamitos, California. A briefer bibliography, together with essays by both friends and critics of the movement, is the reader, *Protest from the Right,* ed. Robert A. Rosenstone (Beverly Hills: The Glencoe Press, 1969).

In combining the historical and the analytical parts of this subject, I have attempted to present a full-length study of the origins, appeal, and influence of fundamentalism of the far right. To the best of my knowledge none of the several books in print on the general radical right are addressed to this subject. Richard Hofstadter has noted, "We need to understand the history of fundamentalism as well as the contributions of depth psychology." [6] This book is a contribution of that understanding.

Rohter, "The Radical Rightists: An Empirical Study," (Ph.D. diss., Michigan State University, 1967), summarized in his article "The Righteous Rightists," *Trans-action,* May, 1967, pp. 27-35; Gary B. Rush, "Status Crystallization and Right Wing Extremist Attitudes," Ph.D. diss., University of Oregon, 1965); the April, 1963, issue of the *Journal of Social Issues* (vol. 19) has several articles by behavioral scientists concerning their difficulties in obtaining data on the far right. See also the useful case studies drawing heavily on behavioral data in *The American Right Wing: Readings in Political Behavior,* ed. Robert A. Schoenberger (New York: Holt, Rinehart, Winston, 1969).

[5] *The Social Psychology of Social Movements* (Indianapolis: Bobbs-Merrill, 1965), p. 198. A good starting point for empirical studies would be a testing of the famous definitions of "intrinsic" and "extrinsic" religion by Prof. Gordon A. Allport, *Personality and Social Encounter: Selected Essays* (Boston: Beacon Press, 1960), p. 257; and Allport and J. Michael Ross, "Personal Religious Orientation and Prejudice," *Journal of Personality and Social Psychology* V (1967), 434.

[6] "Pseudo-Conservatism Revisited: A Postscript," ed. Daniel Bell, *The Radical Right* (Garden City, N. Y.: Doubleday Co., Anchor Books, 1964), p. 103; see also William G. McLoughlin, "Is There a Third Force in Christendom?," in

A major qualification should be made here. This study is not an examination of the religious thought of the entire far right movement. Nor should the reader assume I am suggesting that ultrafundamentalism has been the predominant force in shaping the ideology of the entire radical right. This limitation will explain why I give little attention to some of the more influential far right groups.

What I have done is to show how four individuals and their programs have created "the politics of doomsday." These are:

Dr. Carl McIntire, leader of the American and International Councils of Christian Churches and the Twentieth Century Reformation

Dr. Billy James Hargis, leader of Christian Crusade and member of the International Council of Christian Churches

Mr. (sometimes referred to as "Major") Edgar C. Bundy, leader of the Church League of America and member of the American and International Councils of Christian Churches

Mr. Verne P. Kaub, leader of the American Council of Christian Laymen which merged with the American Council of Christian Churches following Mr. Kaub's death in 1964.

Some readers will wonder why Dr. Fred C. Schwarz and the Christian Anti-Communism Crusade are not included. In its early years that program faithfully followed the ultrafundamentalist position. However in recent years its director has made several important changes. When the total program is evaluated from within the perspective of the far right, it is clear this particular crusade does not meet the full membership requirements. Perhaps Dr. Schwarz does qualify for "honorary membership" as one critic suggests, but on the whole he disassociated himself from most of his earlier colleagues.[7]

Religion in America, eds. McLoughlin and Robert N. Bellah (Boston: Beacon Press, 1968), pp. 60-62, 68-69; the most recent essay, based on careful research, is Dale Leathers, "The Thrust of the Radical Right," ed. Dewitte Holland, *Preaching in American History; Selected Issues in the American Pulpit, 1630-1967* (Nashville: Abingdon Press, 1969), pp. 310-32.

[7] Brooks R. Walker, *The Christian Fright Peddlers* (Garden City, N. Y.: Doubleday & Co., 1964), p. 56; Prof. Koeppen (see note 4 above), who places Schwarz among the far rightists, conducted her interviews with his supporters in

I have quoted extensively from these four spokesmen in the belief that they can best be understood in their own words. I have attempted to avoid painting a black and white picture of their crusade. While I agree wholeheartedly with them that the defense of Christianity and American freedom and resistance to communism are noble goals, I do not believe this means I (or anyone else) should avoid giving their programs extended public consideration. One can find several subversive and antiminority groups, repudiated by the ultrafundamentalists, who also state they are acting on behalf of God and America.

Since we live in an age of great concern about "equal time," some may wonder why no discussion is included of the far left. My primary interest is in the history of American religion in the twentieth century. This book traces the changes in recent times of only one of its branches. Later I hope to probe into the role of the conservatives, moderates, liberals, and radicals in American church life.

The judgments presented here are those of my wife and myself. They should not be considered as representative of any organization, school, or other institution with which we are affiliated. We have received no financial remuneration of any kind from any person, group, council, publisher, or other organization in the preparation of this book other than a generous grant from St. Olaf College for the preparation of the manuscript for the publisher. For those who disagree with our conclusions, we ask that they do not identify these with any other viewpoint than our own.

1962, a time when (it seems to me) Schwarz still linked himself to his ultra-fundamentalist colleagues. By 1965, the cutoff point for my study, he had moved away from his hard-line rightism. See my article on this, "The Remodeled Right: Schwarz and Stormer on Campus," *motive* XXVI (Nov., 1965), 29-32.

1
Foundations, 1920-45

American Protestants in the 1920's found themselves caught up in the concluding chapter of a bitter dispute. For several decades, an increasing number of influential church leaders had been blanding into their theology the most recent findings of biblical scholarship and various shades of evolutionary theory. Their enlarged perspective, in turn, had led many to participate in specific economic and social reform programs.

This new outlook had been roundly denounced by the nation's conservative Protestants. They insisted that no new scholarship or theological reformulation could change the accomplished fact of God's completed revelation as found in the verbally inspired, inerrant Bible. Where reason clashed with biblical faith, men must choose the supernatural revelation of the Scriptures. From the Bible men learned that the church existed to lead men to heaven, not to improve secular society.

By the 1920's the more liberal view had been accepted by most of the influential seminaries and the leaders of the largest denominations. Those remaining loyal to the older tradition had failed repeatedly to hold back the influx of the new theology.

Now, however, the conservative leaders chose to bring together the major doctrines of that heritage as their prime weapons for one supreme battle with the enemy. That counterattack would come to be known as the fundamentalist movement. Its prime resources were pre-millennialism, dispensationalism, verbal inspiration, and religious nationalism. A brief résumé of these teachings will help explain why the struggles of the 1920's proved to be decisive.

In searching for the links of continuity with the past, fundamentalist leaders found their richest resources in the earnest, simple call-to-repentance of Dwight L. Moody. Following in the earlier traditions of American revivals, the famed evangelist of the late nineteenth century had found the words to kindle the devotional zeal of countless Americans and Europeans. In an age of bewildering social and economic change, his followers had found comfort and meaning in his exhortations to repent of their sins, to accept Jesus as their personal Savior, and to live quiet, peaceable lives. When the believer was born again, he received the indwelling power of the Holy Spirit, giving him the strength to overcome evil and to live a godly life.[1]

The momentum for mass revival declined quickly after Moody retired. His younger colleagues—men such as Reuben A. Torrey, A. C. Dixon, and Milan B. Williams—found their supporters united in loyalty to the Bible but divided over theological issues Moody himself had avoided. The most divisive doctrine was that of eschatology: death, resurrection, judgment, and eternity.

To rebut the liberals' contention that no physical Second Coming or eternal life in heaven or hell would ever materialize, conservatives had combed prophetic chapters such as Matthew 24 and 25 and Revelation 19, 20, and 21. Three widely varying interpretations emerged from the search; each reflected a distinctive understanding of what the Bible meant by the "millennium." The premillennialists held that Jesus himself, after physically de-

[1] William G. McLoughlin, *Modern Revivalism: Charles Grandison Finney to Billy Graham* (New York: Ronald Press, 1958), pp. 217-56; Winthrop S. Hudson, *Religion in America* (New York: Charles Scribner's Sons, 1965), chap. 9; James F. Findlay, Jr., *Dwight L. Moody, American Evangelist, 1837-1899* (Chicago: University of Chicago Press, 1969), chap. 7.

feating the Antichrist in war, would reign in bodily form on this planet during the thousand years of perfect peace and then make the Final Judgment. The second school, postmillennialism, taught he would appear bodily to reign at the end of that age. The amillennialists, the third group, argued no literal millennium would be forthcoming. All three did agree that a final judgment day would come, as promised in Matt. 25, when the righteous would inherit heaven, the damned sent to eternal punishment, and this planet destroyed.[2]

Those who later would become fundamentalists accepted the premillennial interpretation because it rested on the principles they used to interpret the Bible. They insisted on an unswerving, literal reading of the Scriptures, even the most difficult passages of Revelation. They rejected any compromise with allegory, symbol, or poetry; that smacked of liberalism, and liberalism was the work of Satan.[3] Post- and amillennialism simply failed their test of biblical truth.

A second major resource for fundamentalists was the school of "dispensationalism." Originating in England among the Plymouth Brethren, the followers sought to understand why God apparently had dealt in different ways with mankind over the centuries. They found seven different "dispensations" or eras in which God had acted differently from before: innocency, conscience, human government, promise, law, grace, and kingdom. The world now stood in the sixth stage; the kingdom promised in Revelation would be the final dispensation.

This interpretation caught on quickly with many conservative Protestants in the later nineteenth century. It seemed scholarly, as evidenced by the "Notes" explaining the seven stages published by Dr. C. I. Scofield. More important, its adherents could use it to prove something they deeply suspected—the Last Days were nearing, the Battle of Armageddon was soon to break out. No wonder the world seemed increasingly im-

[2] Moody himself was premillennial but avoided preaching polemically on the subject; McLoughlin, *Modern Revivalism*, pp. 257-58, 364-99; Findlay, *Dwight L. Moody*, pp. 250-54; Loraine Boettner, *The Millennium* (Philadelphia: The Presbyterian and Reformed Publishing Co., 1958), *passim*.

[3] McLoughlin, *Modern Revivalism*, pp. 257-58, 364-99; see Boettner for a discussion of a further division, "pre" and "post" tribulation rapture, an issue discussed below in relationship to ultrafundamentalism, pp. 130-35.

moral, the church growing apostate, and the people turning to materialism. Dispensationalism explained all this as being part of God's plan, and scores of Protestants believed it.[4]

A third vital ingredient for the growth of fundamentalism appeared in the 1880's under the titles of the "verbal inspiration" and "inerrancy" of the Bible. Again, to refute the increasing acceptance by liberals of an antisupernatural understanding of revelation, conservatives made a fresh, exhaustive statement on the place of the Bible in Christian doctrine. The most important research was conducted at Princeton Theological Seminary by a father and son, Charles and A. A. Hodge, and Benjamin B. Warfield. After careful study Warfield summarized their findings:

> The Church, then has held from the beginning that the Bible is the Word of God in such a sense that its words, though written by men and bearing indelibly impressed upon them the marks of their human origin, were written, nevertheless, under such an influence of the Holy Ghost as to be also the words of God, the adequate expression of His mind and will. It has always recognized that this conception of co-authorship implies that the Spirit's superintendence extends to the choice of the words by the human authors [verbal inspiration], and preserves its product from everything inconsistent with divine authorship—thus securing, among other things, that entire truthfulness which is everywhere presupposed in and asserted for Scripture by the Biblical writers [inerrancy].[5]

Conceding that ambiguities and puzzles did exist as to the precise meaning of certain passages, the Princeton scholars stated that such problems resulted from faulty translations and mis-

---

[4] McLoughlin, *Modern Revivalism*, pp. 257-58, 364-99; among the many studies see especially C. Norman Kraus, *Dispensationalism in America: Its Rise and Development* (Richmond: John Knox Press, 1958).

[5] B. B. Warfield, *The Inspiration and Authority of the Bible*, ed. Samuel G. Craig (Philadelphia: The Presbyterian and Reformed Publishing Co., 1949), p. 173; A. A. Hodge and B. B. Warfield, "Inspiration," *Presbyterian Review*, II (1881), 225-38; for a full discussion on how this school differs from the Westminster Confession see Ernest R. Sandeen, "The Princeton Theology," *Church History*, XXXI (September, 1962), 307-21.

copying over the centuries. In the original manuscript form, the "autographa" or first edition contained no "errors" because God had directly and verbally (but not mechanically) told each author what to write. Since God could not err, his written revelation to men was inerrant. Each word was equally inspired; none could be deleted, no additional words were needed.

God acted in such a way that the authors knew they were speaking by his full authority, as stated in the proof text, 2 Timothy 3:14-17. These words were considered to be definitive, external evidence of the final, indestructible norm God had given man for assessing theological truth and error. The internal evidence of man's own personal religious experience must be measured against that criterion. Pure doctrine rather than personal encounter became the only standard of all religious truth. Salvation was still by faith through grace alone, to be sure, but now faith meant loyalty to those absolute truths God commanded men to believe. Those who professed these doctrines were Christians, those who showed any reluctance or questioning were not.[6]

Sensing an imminent victory over the liberals and eager to win new converts, Torrey and Dixon prepared a massive publication program. Finding substantial support, in 1910 they solicited and edited dozens of articles from theologically orthodox scholars, clergymen, and laity in several countries spelling out the richness and breadth of their faith. Within the next few years they published a total of twelve volumes under the title of *The Fundamentals: A Testimony to the Truth*. In all, over three million copies were distributed throughout the world.

The Fundamentals helped greatly in building the momentum soon to appear as the fundamentalist movement. The contributors examined the full range of Christian concern: biblical studies, theology, ethics, missions, stewardship, personal witness, and the problems raised by science. Within a few years these works would be recognized as the best evidence in print of the vitality of conservative Protestantism.[7]

[6] See again Sandeen, "The Princeton Theology," and his "Toward a Historical Interpretation of the Origins of Fundamentalism," *Church History*, XXXVI (March, 1967), 66-83.

[7] Published in Chicago (n.d.) by the Testimony Publishing Company; reprinted in two volumes as *The Fundamentals for Today*, ed. Charles L. Feinberg (Grand Rapids: Kregel Publications, 1958), and a one volume edition in 1961.

The enthusiasm for orthodoxy kindled by these volumes appeared just at the time World War I broke out. Suddenly, almost overnight, the fourth element of the fundamentalism of the 1920's, religious nationalism, entered into the mainstream of conservative theology. Both British propagandists and American preachers such as Billy Sunday, W. B. Riley, and George McCready Price, told American churchgoers that Satan himself was directing the German war effort. Had not Germany harbored those liberal critics who rejected the God of the Bible? Were not the Huns killing women and children? What else could you expect from a nation which had rejected Christianity? The preachers rejoiced when America joined the Allies in April, 1917; God had led this nation into war. He would use it to restore the true faith among all peoples.[8]

The same spokesmen readily grafted the Bolshevik Revolution of 1917 onto the main branch of their argument. In their judgment, that upheaval exposed the presence of a diabolically clever world conspiracy made up of Kaiserism, evolutionism, Bolshevism, higher criticism, and liberal theology. All were of the same cloth since all would overturn Christian institutions and make this world the Devil's paradise. To combat such power, these spokesmen demanded that every citizen exhibit "100% Americanism"; any deviation from their standards of patriotism was adequate proof of near-treasonous activity.[9]

The preaching of Billy Sunday, former baseball player and spellbinder supreme, met with extraordinary popularity during and after the war. His religious thought, unsystematic and formless to be sure, was nonetheless a blending of premillennialism, verbal inspiration, and religious nationalism.

Billy Sunday recognized that Americans in the 1920's worried deeply over the failure of Prohibition, corruption in politics, increasing crime, Sacco and Vanzetti, socialist clergymen, and the teaching of evolution. There seemed so little the good people

---

[8] Norman F. Furniss, *The Fundamentalist Controversy, 1918-31* (New Haven: Yale University Press, 1954), pp. 23-27. A classic presentation of the anti-German argument is William B. Riley, *The Menace of Modernism* (New York: Christian Alliance Publishing Company, 1917).

[9] Riley, *Menace,* and George McCready Price, *Poisoning Democracy: A Study of the Moral and Religious Aspects of Socialism* (Westwood, N. J.: Fleming H. Revell, 1921).

could do to stop it all. Sunday spoke to that concern, dazzling his audiences with the kind of freewheeling, biting, antiliberal, antiintellectual speeches they wanted to hear. Through him they could strike back at the bad people: liberals, higher critics, evolutionists, and less-than-100 percenters.[10]

Sunday's outlook foreshadowed much of the religious nationalism of today's ultrafundamentalism. To cite a few parallels, he had no doubts that America was the one truly Christian nation in the world; hence only it could defend pure Christian doctrine. He linked religious liberalism to Bolshevism in finding a link between Dr. Harry Emerson Fosdick and "the garlic-smelling, bomb-throwing, unassimilated immigrant." He believed Trotsky and Lenin had promulgated liberal theology. He freely linked the Federal Council of Churches with communism, delighting in drawing up lists of those individuals he deemed unsafe for the security of the church and America.[11]

Although Sunday was unpopular with some conservatives, he had won the enthusiastic support of those committed to premillennialism and verbal inspiration. This was made abundantly clear when some 6,500 Protestants convened in Philadelphia in 1919 for a national witness to their faith. Joined by other firebrand revivalists—such as Gerald Winrod, W. B. Riley, and Paul Rader—Sunday and the delegates adopted a "Statement of Belief" for the newly-created "World Christian Fundamentalist Association." In essence, the delegates again reaffirmed that only by total loyalty to propositional doctrine could one become a born-again Christian.[12]

Buoyed by the popularity of the revivalists, the enthusiasm

[10] Richard Hofstadter, Anti-Intellectualism in American Life (New York: Alfred A. Knopf, 1963), pp. 114-19; Robert K. Murray, Red Scare: A Study in National Hysteria, 1919-1920 (Minneapolis: University of Minnesota Press, 1955), chap. 6.

[11] William G. McLoughlin, Billy Sunday Was His Real Name (Chicago: University of Chicago Press, 1955), chap. 4 and pp. 279-83; Hofstadter, Anti-Intellectualism, pp. 118-19; Ned B. Stonehouse presents a less critical view in J. Gresham Machen: A Memoir (Grand Rapids: Eerdmans Publishing Co., 1954), pp. 222-28.

[12] The "Statement of Belief" is in Carrol Edwin Harrington, "The Fundamentalist Movement in America, 1870-1920," (Ph.D. diss., Berkeley: University of California, 1959), chap. 14; W. B. Riley, "The Faith of a Fundamentalist," Current History, XXIV (June, 1927), 434-40.

of the Philadelphia rally, and the assurance that only their theology harmonized with the will of God, the fundamentalists in the early 1920's forced their adversaries into battle. While the intensity and scope of combat varied among the denominations involved, most groups had to wrestle with the same general issues. The fundamentalists demanded public tests of orthodoxy for seminary professors and clergymen; they called for the resignation of dissenting church journal editors; they demanded that public schools ban the teaching of evolution; and they petitioned rank and file members to support their plans to remove any suspected liberals from denominational office.

The battle which would lead directly to the appearance of ultrafundamentalism in the 1950's took place within the nation's largest Presbyterian body, the Presbyterian Church, U.S.A. Having lost one of the denomination's two seminaries, Union of New York, to the liberals years ago, conservative Presbyterians now united to preserve the orthodoxy of the faculty at Princeton Theological Seminary. If Princeton fell, they believed, the war and indeed true Christianity would be lost.

The New Jersey school had maintained a faculty of conservatives throughout the early years of the battle. Then a new president, Dr. J. Ross Stevenson, suggested a wider theological outlook among future faculty appointees. The conservatives interpreted this as a declaration of war. They found their leader and their ammunition in a gifted young New Testament scholar at the seminary, Dr. J. Gresham Machen. Devoted to verbal inspiration, inerrancy, and the Westminster Confession, he had by vigorous teaching and impressive scholarship, primarily his book *Christianity and Liberalism* of 1923, staked out the terrain for battle: no liberals on the faculty, no liberal seminarians ordained, no liberals on the schools' board of directors. Anything less than this would be the surrender of the Christian faith.[18]

[18] Lefferts A. Loetscher, *The Broadening Church: A Study of Theological Issues in the Presbyterian Church Since 1869* (Philadelphia: University of Pennsylvania Press, 1954), chaps. 6-9, 13; Dallas Morgan Roark, "J. Gresham Machen and His Desire to Maintain a Doctrinally True Presbyterian Church," (Ph.D. diss., University of Iowa, 1963), [hereafter cited as Roark, "Machen" Dissertation]; he has summarized his study in a two-part article, "J. Gresham Machen," *Journal of Presbyterian History*, XLIII (June, Sept., 1965), 124-38, 174-81 [hereafter cited as Roark, "Machen" *Presbyterian History*, XLIII]. See

Machen attracted strong support, but in battle after battle he failed to convince the final arbiter, the General Assembly of the church, to obey his ultimatum. Liberals were appointed to the board, liberal seminarians were ordained, liberal ministers were not censured. After some five years of intensive wrangling and often bitter personal polemics on all sides, Machen gave in. Convinced after losing every contest that Princeton now could not be saved, he and two close associates resigned. They refused to yield on verbal inspiration: either the Bible was totally inerrant and verbally inspired, or it was merely some Jewish mythology; specific doctrines were completely true or completely false; true Christian fellowship could not be carried on with those dedicated to the perpetuation of apostasy. To preserve the great historic doctrines of the faith, Machen insisted, the true Christian must separate from the modernists, the liberals, and, yes, the moderates. Only a saving remnant of the orthodox could carry on God's will on earth until the Final Judgment when their labors would be rewarded.

In 1929 the dissenting Princeton professors and several students moved to Philadelphia and established Westminster Theological Seminary. Such a split was not uncommon among some of the larger Protestant bodies in the late 1920's.[14] The founding of Westminster, however, took on a unique meaning. It would become a decisive step in the formation of ultrafundamentalism because one of the students to follow Machen was Carl McIntire. He more than any other individual would establish the ideology, the tone, and the momentum for fundamentalism of the far right. His leadership would become paramount.

Born in 1906 in Ypsilanti, Michigan, McIntire earned a teacher's certificate at Southeastern State Teacher's College, Oklahoma, and in 1927 a B.A. degree from Park College, Missouri. After choosing the ministry for his career, he entered Princeton Seminary. He was elected president of his junior (or first-year) class. He was deeply attracted to the teaching of Machen, writing later that the professor's lectures had inspired him to enter into

---

also David C. Jones, "Machen's Ecclesiology," *The Presbyterian Guardian,* XXXII (Oct., 1963), 134, 139; Stonehouse, *Machen,* pp. 364-70.

[14] Roark, "Machen" Dissertation, pp. 112-19; Roark, "Machen," *Presbyterian History,* XLIII, 133-34; the most detailed account of the events in the 1920's is in Stonehouse, *Machen;* Carl McIntire, *The Death of a Church* (Collingswood, N. J.: Christian Beacon Press, 1967), chap. 15.

"the conflicts of the day." He followed his mentor to Westminster in 1929; it was the first of several separations which would characterize his career.[15]

The Westminster faculty and student body soon started a program of bold, often bitter criticism of their parent church and the Federal Council of Churches to which it belonged. In 1932, they found in a pamphlet published by the FCC, "The Social Ideas of the Church," ideas they deemed tantamount to communism. Convinced that American capitalism was as divinely approved as the Westminster Confession, they drew up a complete indictment of the denomination and the council. In the same year they uncovered what to them was even more diabolic evidence; in China the Presbyterian and Federal Council missionaries were converting the local residents to communism.[16]

Churchmen could argue forever about theology but the Presbyterian Church, U.S.A., was not about to ignore the charge of being pro-Communist. After listening in 1933 to Machen's charges, the General Assembly voted its Board of Foreign Missions its "wholehearted, unequivocal, enthusiastic, and affectionate commendation." [17] That decision, just as Machen's indictment, was an irrevocable ultimatum. Neither side could now compromise; neither side wanted to compromise.

The Machenites now unfurled the flag of open rebellion. Remaining members of the denomination, they established within that body itself their own Independent Board of Foreign Missions, although no constitutional provision for such a body existed. They went so far as to ask congregations to support their program and to withhold funds from the official board. McIntire actively sup-

[15] The official biography is a booklet, Clarence Laman, "God Calls a Man" (Collingswood, N. J.: Christian Beacon Press, 1959). McIntire graduated from Westminster in 1931, served two years in a Presbyterian Church, U.S.A., parish in Atlantic City and then moved to Collingswood where he remains.

[16] The communism charge is in a pamphlet by an ACCC leader, Dr. Robert E. Kofahl, "History and Testimony of the Bible Presbyterian Church" (n.d., n.p.); *Christian Beacon*, June 3, 1965, p. 7; John A. Stroman, "The American Council of Christian Churches" (Ph.D. diss., Boston University, 1966), pp. 67-68; *Re-thinking Missions: A Laymen's Inquiry After One Hundred Years*, ed. William E. Hocking et al. (New York: Harper and Brothers, 1932); Loetscher, *The Broadening Church*, pp. 149-56; Roark, "Machen," *Presbyterian History* XLIlII, 134-35; McIntire, *Death of a Church*, pp. 144-45.

[17] Roark, "Machen," *Presbyterian History* XLIII, 135; Roark, "Machen" Dissertation, p. 122.

ported the insurgents and wrote later that although the board was "outside the control and authority of the General Assembly," it had been established by the authority of Jesus Christ.[18]

The leaders of the Presbyterian Church, U.S.A., swiftly insisted that the Independent Board make clear its true intentions; dissent was one thing and calculated disruption was quite another. The officials stated that those choosing to remain members of the denomination would have to respect the authorized agencies of that body; they pointed out this was a well-known prerequisite to prospective members. Those who did not wish to show this respect were free to resign.[19]

No resignations from the Westminster faction appeared. The appropriate Presbytery of the denomination then initiated formal proceedings to remove the members of the Independent Board from membership in the church. Again, no one resigned. Indeed, Machen, McIntire, and the others appealed their case up through the official review channels of the denomination. In May, 1963, the final arbiter, the General Assembly, dismissed Dr. Machen from membership.[20] They next rejected the appeal of the Rev. McIntire and dismissed him from membership.

Six charges against the Collingswood, New Jersey, minister had been considered by the review board:

1. Disapproval, defiance, and acts in contravention of the government and discipline of the Presbyterian Church, U.S.A.; 2. Not being zealous and faithful in maintaining the peace of the Church; 3. Contempt of and rebellion against his brethren in the Church; 4. Conduct unbecoming a minister of the Gospel; 5. Advocating rebellion against the con-

[18] McIntire, Death of a Church, pp. 144-45; Loetscher, The Broadening Church, chap. 15; Stroman, "The American Council," pp. 69-74.

[19] Stonehouse, Machen, pp. 489-99; Minutes of the General Assembly of 1934, pp. 69-71, and 1936, Part I, p. 92; Roark, "Machen" Dissertation, pp. 126-35; McIntire, Twentieth Century Reformation, rev. ed. (Collingswood, N. J.: Christian Beacon Press, 1945), p. 211; in Death of a Church, pp. 144-48, McIntire argues that the proceedings from the outset were unconstitutional; Christian Beacon, June 10, 1965, pp. 2-3, July 16, 1959, p. 3, May 3, 1962, p. 2.

[20] McIntire, Death of a Church, pp. 148-62; New York Times, May 30, 1936, p. 32; see the account of the trial in The Reformed Presbyterian Reporter XCIX (June, 1965), pp. 9-10.

stituted authorities of the Church; 6. Violation of his ordination vows.[21]

Of these, the assembly accepted Charges 1, 2, and 6 as the basis for the dismissal. The other charges were set aside.

The objections by the General Assembly to the Independent Board were stated in precise terms:

> These offenses enumerated in the cases against these men were specifically against the moral law. The Presbyterian Church determined that it must defend its loyal ministers and members who were defamed and its agencies who were being opposed. In bringing the offenders to trial and in inflicting upon them defnite censures for their offenses, the Presbyterian Church took the only resourse that it was possible for it to take to exonerate the innocent ministers and lawful agencies upon whom the offenders were heaping unmerited abuse and malicious slander.[22]

McIntire replied to these charges:

> Our defense was simple. We were not in defiance of the government and discipline of the Presbyterian Church because the consitution itself provided that "God alone is lord of the conscience, and hath left it free from the doctrines and commandments of men which are in any thing contrary to his Word, or beside it, in matters of faith or worship."

In his judgment, "we were not guilty of sin before the Head of the Church." [23]

This event would become decisive in the career of the thirty-year-old New Jersey clergyman. It would lead him to find

[21] These are cited by McIntire in *Death of a Church*, p. 152; in his *Twentieth Century Reformation*, p. 211, he stated ". . . we were unfrocked . . ."; see the *Minutes of the General Assembly of 1936*, Part I, pp. 92 ff.

[22] This is found in a publication of the Presbyterian Church, U.S.A., "A Statement" (1936); for other critical views, liberal and conservative, see the editorial comment cited by Ralph Lord Roy, *Apostles of Discord* (Boston: Beacon Press, 1953), pp. 189-90.

[23] McIntire, *Death of a Church*, p. 152; McIntire, *Servants of Apostasy* (Collingswood, N. J.: Christian Beacon Press, 1955), p. 384; for a detailed discussion see Jones, "Machen's Ecclesiology," *Presbyterian Guardian* XXXII (Oct., 1963), 134-36, 138-43.

in what became known as total separation the criterion by which he would assess every phase of Christian thought and practice. Nothing less than complete allegiance to its demands would satisfy his zeal for doctrinal conformity. So deep was this commitment that only its heartfelt intensity can help explain a profound paradox in McIntire's judgment. If total separation were clearly God's command to all Christians, and if (as he wrote), "Christ walks that road, too," then it would seem that those deposed in 1936 would have voluntarily left the church body they had already found to be officially apostate. Rather they had used every constitutional means available to maintain membership within the parent church.[24]

From any perspective, however, it is clear that the dismissal gave McIntire the opportunity to point to his own experience as evidence that he was loyal to his convictions. This would establish him, in the eyes of his followers, as qualified to lead a "Twentieth Century Reformation." In the hands of his critics, however, the dismissal would be ample proof that he was a disruptive force and maker of schisms.

After the final appeal to the General Assembly was rejected, the deposed ministers and some three hundred lay Presbyterians met in Philadelphia in June, 1936, to organize "The Presbyterian Church of America." They envisaged it as a biblically pure denomination, physically free from any need to touch apostasy.[25]

The exhilarating hopes for a doctrinally uniform church proved illusory. Freed from having to keep closed ranks against the common enemy, the Presbyterian Church, U.S.A., the strong-willed separationists started arguing frequently and bitterly among themselves. Machen insisted, in the first dispute, that premillennialism in itself was not contrary to biblical eschatology, but he

[24] This is suggested In a criticism of the ACCC by a past president of the National Association of Evangelicals, Stephen W. Paine, in a booklet, " 'Separation' is Separating Evangelicals" (Boston: Fellowship Press, 1951), p. 5. Paine implies that the choice of practicing total separation was making a virtue out of necessity. McIntire replies to this in a booklet, "The Testimony of Separation," chap. 8 (Collingswood, N. J.: Christian Beacon Press, 1952).

[25] Machen, Stonehouse, chap. 25; Edward L. Kellogg, "Lest We Forget," a pamphlet of the Orthodox Presbyterian Church (n.d.), p. 3; Stroman "The American Council," pp. 82-84; see a sermon on the founding by Gordon H. Clark in The Reformed Presbyterian Reporter XCIX (June, 1965), 9-12.

31

firmly rejected the dispensationalism espoused by many within the new church. McIntire quickly took exception. Through the pages of his weekly journal, *The Christian Beacon,* he insisted each congregation should have full "eschatological liberty" for its doctrinal standards. This was his first public break with his mentor.[26]

The dissident Presbyterians soon found themselves embroiled in a second and much more explosive issue, the private use of alcoholic beverages. McIntire demanded that any use be denied members of the Westminster Seminary faculty. The teachers took deep exception to his charges with the implication of excessive use. As with dispensationalism, no one would agree on a solution. The only apparent result was more suspicion and more division within the frail young church.[27]

A third issue, the wording of several amendments for the proposed constitution of the denomination, brought the smoldering factionalism into clear view in late 1936. Both McIntire and the Westminster staff proposed separate sets of amendments. At the General Assembly meeting both sides criticized and often attacked the other in terms reminiscent of the old Foreign Missions Board uproar. In the final vote McIntire's proposals were rejected; the young denomination's first assembly concluded on an extremely sour note of personality conflict.[28]

Whatever harmony still remained after these battles now vanished at the year's end. The McIntire group published a detailed, searching criticism of the theology of some Westminster professors. They also organized an anti-Machen movement within the missions board, gaining enough strength to defeat Machen for the presidency even though he had filed for reelection. The removal was not without irony. The original spokesman and prime

[26] Machen, *Christianity and Liberalism* (New York: Macmillan, 1923), p. 49; *Christian Beacon,* July 16, 1959, pp. 2, 3; Roark, "Machen" Dissertation, pp. 134-41. The most complete account is in a series of four articles by George Marsden, "Perspective on the Division of 1937," *The Presbyterian Guardian* XXXIII (Jan.-April, 1964); most of my account is drawn from these four articles. C. C. Ryrie, *Dispensationalism Today* (Chicago: Moody Press, 1964), p. 80 states that the ACCC is officially nondispensational.
[27] See Marsden, "Perspective," Feb., 1964, pp. 27-29; *Christian Beacon,* July 16, 1959, pp. 3, 4.
[28] The issues here are exceedingly complicated; the best guide is in the work by Marsden, especially the Feb., 1964, issue, pp. 28-29; see also Roark, "Machen" Dissertation, p. 137, and Stonehouse, *Machen,* pp. 503-4.

mover for total separation now found himself separated from the movement he had virtually singlehandedly created. Machen attempted to rebuild support by visiting friends throughout the country. When in North Dakota in late December, he was struck by pneumonia and died on New Year's Day.[29]

The first months of 1937 found the separatists unable to find common ground between the McIntire and Westminster factions. By the summer everyone seemed resigned to the fact that they had no course left but to divide again. Most of the Westminster group organized the "Orthodox Presbyterian Church," and the McIntire wing established the "Bible Presbyterian Church." Both claimed to be the sole American custodian of historic Presbyterianism and the Westminster Confession. Neither made serious overtures toward reconciliation. The Bible Presbyterians organized their own school, Faith Theological Seminary. Most of the denomination's finances came from McIntire's congregation of 1,200 members in Collingswood.[30]

The 1937 separation among the separationists in essence created ultrafundamentalism because it freed the Rev. McIntire, the undisputed leader of the anti-Machen faction, of any need for conciliatory action towards any with whom he and his followers differed. Those who remained supported him without reservation. From this base, tiny and virtually unnoticed by the general public, he introduced into his writing and preaching a judgment which would later become crucial to his "Twentieth Century Reformation" and thus to ultrafundamentalism. Rather than joining those nonseparated, conservative church leaders who were denouncing the familiar ills in America (drinking, gambling, swearing, cinema, dancing, smoking, and the like), McIntire instead spent the overwhelming amount of his time attacking those church people who were not members of the Bible Presbyterian Church. That group

[29] Stonehouse, *Machen*, pp. 504-5; *Christian Beacon*, July 16, 1959, p. 2; Marsden, "Perspective," Feb., 1964, p. 29; Roark presents evidence suggesting Machen's physician believed the shock of defeat was so great as to leave him in a weakened physical condition and thus more vulnerable to illness; Roark, "Machen," *Presbyterian History* XLIII, p. 138; Marsden, "Perspective," March, 1964, pp. 43-45.

[30] See McIntire's account in *Death of a Church*, pp. 164-74, which includes the Articles of Association and the first resolutions; McIntire, *Servants*, p. 358; *Christian Beacon*, March 25, 1965, p. 5; Stroman, "The American Council," pp. 85-89.

included somewhat over 99 percent of all American church members. McIntire argued, "as the church goes, so goes the nation." He cast himself as a reformer in the Luther-Calvin mold. He reasoned that since only he and his followers presented a pure witness, *only* they were God's representatives to preserve Christianity; everyone else was apostate.

Nowhere did McIntire find apostasy more rampant than in the Federal Council of Churches. Deeply resenting its vast prestige, its openness towards experimentation in its programs, and its refusal to require doctrinal conformity of its members, he chose to build his reformation on an anticouncil foundation.

In a manner remarkably close to Machen's indictment of the Presbyterian Church, U.S.A., the Rev. McIntire drew up a bill of charges against the Federal Council. First, the FCC was antibiblical because it refused to promulgate a formal doctrinal creed. Second, the council gave aid and comfort to communism because its ranks included some members of front groups. Third, the FCC enjoyed an immoral monopoly in radio programming because it was the only church agency consulted by the Federal Communications Commission concerning the content of the free broadcasting which it required of the nation's stations. Finally, McIntire objected to the policy of the Armed Forces in recruiting chaplains only from the ranks of the Federal Council denominations.[81]

The New Jersey clergyman realized that a stand for pure doctrine alone would not bring on any reformation; he needed publicity, he needed members, and he needed money. In 1940, word came that a nearby separationist group had left the national Methodist Church and organized the "Bible Protestant Church." As was true of his group, the membership was only a few thousand, but McIntire found their doctrine and plans for the future harmonized very closely with the Bible Presbyterians. The two

[81] Herbert W. Schneider, *Religion in Twentieth-Century America* (Cambridge: Harvard University Press, 1952), pp. 77-79; Ralph Lord Roy, *Communism and the Churches* (New York: Harcourt, Brace, 1960), pp. 227-28; Roy, *Apostles of Discord,* pp. 40-43; McIntire, *Twentieth Century Reformation,* chap. 2; McIntire, *The Rise of the Tyrant* (Collingswood, N. J.: Christian Beacon Press, 1945), chap. 5; the standard history of the FCC is John A. Hutchison, *We Are Not Divided* (New York: Round Table Press, 1941); Louis Gasper, *The Fundamentalist Movement* (The Hague; Mouton and Company, 1963), p. 24; a summary by the ACCC is its Literature Item no. 300, "The American Council of Christian Churches."

groups explored the possibilities of forming a council to provide a common witness and a more powerful barrier to the Federal Council's influence in the nation's religious life. In 1941, the leaders created the American Council of Christian Churches with a membership of some 40,000, located mainly in the mid-Atlantic seaboard states. They took their stand:

To Provide A Pure Testimony For Fundamental Churches.

To Facilitate Cooperation Among True Christian Churches.

To Project A United Stand Against Religious Modernism.

To Expose Communist Infiltration Into The Church.

To Oppose Every System Alien To The Bible

To Proclaim Unashamedly The Whole Council Of God.[32]

While the new council reflected the new-born religious thought of ultrafundamentalism, it failed to attract any significant number of the nation's conservative Protestants. Most of these looked hopefully towards the progress being made by another group exploring the possibilities for some new federation to oppose the power of the Federal Council of Churches. After informal negotiations, delegates from several independent denominations met in April, 1942, in St. Louis, Missouri, and laid the base for what would become the National Association of Evangelicals. McIntire, the ACCC president, outlined the terms by which that council would associate with the proposed group. He left no doubts but that the terms would include total separation; no member could have any dealing with an agency or individual associated in any manner with the Federal Council.

The majority of delegates looked at the issue in a different light. Agreeing with McIntire that a true Christian must always resist apostasy, they believed this could be done by a person working for sound doctrine inside the denomination to which he belonged, which might be a member of the Federal Council. A Christian could and should work from within, and not simply stand outside and condemn. Membership in a denomination which had some dealings with the Federal Council did not automatically mean (as McIntire had insisted) that the individual accepted any

[32] Most ACCC pamphlets print this statement, see Literature Item No. 300; McIntire, *Twentieth Century Reformation,* pp. 11-14, 179-82; a complete account of the forming of the ACCC is in Stroman, "The American Council," chap. 4.

or all of the doctrine of some other members of that council. The majority of the proposed association founders concluded that each Christian should have the opportunity to decide for himself when he must separate from apostasy. To them, this kind of personal choice was one of the great triumphs of the Protestant Reformation and they wanted it preserved.[33]

When the final vote was called the delegates chose not to associate with the American Council of Christian Churches. The outcome did not displease the president of the ACCC; he had left St. Louis with the purity of his council still unscathed.

The failure of the fundamentalists to unite in 1942 pointed up the problems faced by the heirs of Dwight L. Moody in the mid-twentieth century. Where once the orthodox stood proudly together in the midst of a great revival, their descendants could now only argue bitterly with one another. The best of Moody's evangelism—its warmth, its irenic temper, and its openness to responsible scholarship, such as the Princeton theology—had hardened into bitter doctrinal acrimony.

What the fundamentalists of the early 1940's had not resolved was what to do when an inerrant text does not clarify honest differences of interpretation among its adherents. The conservatives after Moody had agreed to disagree on some of the issues; dispensationalism, pre- and posttribulation rapture, and even pre- and postmillennialism. But they all realized no compromise could be made on verbal inerrancy; they all agreed there was no substitute for sound Scriptural doctrine. But did the Bible teach total separation as understood by Carl McIntire? Many conservatives thought not, and on that issue the heirs of Moody chose to battle among themselves rather than unite against the common foe.

Those joining the ACCC became the "ultrafundamentalists." They identified with the great doctrines of Protestant orthodoxy and with verbal inspiration, but they insisted on total separation as well. By 1942, their movement was only a few years old, but

[33] Bruce Shelley, *Evangelicalism in America: Its Rise and Development* (Grand Rapids: Eerdmans Publishing Co., 1968), pp. 80-83; James DeForest Murch, *Cooperation Without Compromise: A History of the National Association of Evangelicals* (Grand Rapids: Eerdmans Publishing Co., 1956), pp. 51-56; McIntire, "Testimony of Separation," chap. 7; McLoughlin, *Modern Revivalism,* pp. 475-78.

most of its distinctive traits were already visible—a zeal for engaging in polemical disputation, a confidence that man's rationality could formulate and grasp the full depth of biblical truth expressed as propositional doctrine, a deep suspicion of all who seemed less than enthusiastic about total separation, and a conviction that the great crises facing America could be traced back directly to galloping apostasy in its churches. What America needed, what the world needed, was a Twentieth Century Reformation.

The fundamentalist tradition survived the breach at St. Louis. At the time the delegates were meeting, new forces appeared throughout the world which would revitalize the American Council, the Federal Council, and the National Association of Evangelicals alike. The world was at war in 1942. From that holocaust would emerge the ingredient needed by the ultrafundamentalists to complete their plans for reforming America. That ingredient would be 'the politics of doomsday.'

2
Renewal and Expansion, 1945-57

The radio announcers had been hinting all day that the long-awaited news would be released momentarily. As the world listened, the suspense was prolonged by the solemn tolling at midnight of Big Ben. Prime Minister Clement Atlee stated the joyous news: Japan had surrendered unconditionally; World War II had ended.

This was a day for celebration, for thanksgiving, and for pondering the future. For all the overwhelming relief peace had brought, it could not cover over the many ominous events of that year—the millions of casualties, the discovery of the crematoriums, the implications of nuclear warfare, and the sudden hostility of the Soviet allies. Americans on V-J Day found cause to wonder and worry, if only a little, about the postwar world.

Among those who reflected on the future were four men, then unknown to one another and scarcely known outside their immediate communities. Outwardly it seemed as though they shared little in common; they differed widely in age, level of education, profession, and region. Within fifteen years, however, they would become the most influential leaders in a religiously-oriented action program commanding six- and seven-figure budgets, sponsoring daily radio porgrams over a thousand stations, and molding the ideals and fears of tens of thousands of citizens. These men would become recognized as the leaders of fundamentalism of the far right. Their several differences would be submerged in the cause of their common interest in the American and International Councils of Christian Churches and their loyalty to the religious nationalism most fully expressed by Dr. Carl McIntire.

Before 1958, the leadership contributed by the New Jersey clergyman would be largely responsible for the appearance of four independent but related enterprises; his Twentieth Century Reformation; the Church League of America headed by Edgar C. Bundy, who in 1945 was an Army Air Force officer and an ordained Southern Baptist minister; the Christian Crusade led by Dr. Billy James Hargis, then a twenty-year-old evangelist in rural Oklahoma; and the American Council of Christian Laymen founded after 1945 by Mr. Verne Paul Kaub, who on V-J Day was a public relations consultant for the Wisconsin Power and Light Company.

This chapter describes the rise to leadership of these men. The narrative, divided into three parts, is not strictly chronological. The first part sketches the conflicts among fundamentalists from 1945 to 1957; the second returns to 1945 to review briefly the phases of the cold war which led to the prominence of Senator Joseph R. McCarthy; the third is an account of the emergence of ultrafundamentalism as a distinct ecclesiastical movement and also as one part of the crusade which, after 1958, would become the far right.

Following the surrender of the Axis powers, American society underwent many profound transformations, including the well-known religious revival of the late 1940's and early 1950's. That movement is too familiar to require retelling here. However, one of its chief features contributed heavily to the appearance of fundamentalism of the far right. After 1945, the great majority of conservative Protestants showed little interest in the internecine controversies set off at St. Louis in 1942 between the National Association of Evangelicals and the American Council of Christian Churches. Rather, they vigorously supported the interdenominational evangelism of Youth for Christ, Inter-Varsity Christian Fellowship, and the preaching of Billy Graham. Not since the great days of Dwight L. Moody had so many Americans been so enthusiastic about a revivalist preacher.

The popularity of these new programs was due, in large part, to the success of their leaders in presenting a straightforward call to repentance without falling back into the divisive pitfalls of the fundamentalist-modernist controversy of an earlier day. One of the early spokesmen, Dr. Harold John Ockenga, deplored the "fragmentation, segregation, separation, criticism, censoriousness, suspicion, [and] solecism" of the fundamentalists and called for a greater social awareness of the great crises facing the postwar world.[1]

Momentum for a revitalized social ethic among conservatives continued to grow. Gradually, without so much as a national conference or even a committee meeting being convened, a new movement among American Protestants came into existence. At first its leaders called it "neo-evangelicalism"; later this became "the new evangelicalism." Its supporters were "evangelicals" rather than "fundamentalists."

The movement soon attracted support from publishing houses, colleges, seminaries, and Bible institutes; it encouraged new journals and Sunday school curricula. Although differing in certain details, the new evangelicalism came to work closely with the program and witness of the National Association of Evangelicals.[2]

At the same time, the ecumenical-minded churchmen of America and the world were themselves moving quickly toward the achievement of their long-standing goal of global unity. At a meeting in Amsterdam in 1948, representatives of 147 churches from 44 nations established the World Council of Churches. From the outset it denied the charge that it aimed at establishing

[1] Ockenga writing in *Christian Life,* June 1947, pp. 13-15; the most important study of the new movement is Carl F. H. Henry, *The Uneasy Conscience of Modern Fundamentalism* (Grand Rapids: Eerdmans Publishing Co., 1947); McLoughlin, *Modern Revivalism,* pp. 472-82.

[2] Millard Erickson, *The New Evangelical Theology* (Westwood, N. J.: Fleming H. Revell, 1968); Ronald H. Nash, *The New Evangelicalism* (Grand Rapids: Zondervan Publishing House, 1963); Gasper, *The Fundamentalist Movement;* Daniel B. Stevick, *Beyond Fundamentalism* (Richmond: John Knox Press, 1964); Shelley, *Evangelicalism in America.*

a "superchurch"; its unity would be spiritual rather than organic.

The appearance of the World Council was interpreted by both the American Council and the National Association of Evangelicals as the most serious threat ever faced by traditional Christianity. That council, in their judgment, embraced inclusivism, liberalism, members from Communist nations, critics of capitalism (as well as of communism), and militant apostates. If it would continue to grow, the WCC could obliterate the cherished loyalties of the many independent church bodies supporting the ACCC or the NAE.

Yet, despite the fact that they understood the WCC was their common enemy, the leaders of the National Association and the American Council refused to join together for a joint witness of resistance. Neither side made any overture at reconciliation. Instead, McIntire and some fifty like-minded churchmen from America and abroad met in Amsterdam and established the International Council of Christian Churches just prior to the WCC meeting. Its doctrinal statement was the same as that of the ACCC. Its stated purpose was to harass and oppose the World Council, just as the American Council existed to oppose the Federal Council of Churches.

The creation of the ICCC attracted considerable publicity since most newsmen who were in Amsterdam to report the WCC knew little of the history of separationist criticism of ecumenicity. They found the International Council spokesmen were generously issuing the kind of copy that made news, such as labeling the proposed WCC as a tool of Moscow and an anti-Christian organization. Undoubtedly many readers of the major American daily papers now heard of the McIntire-led movement for the first time.[3]

With both a national and worldwide organization under his leadership, McIntire in the late 1940's intensified his criticism of everyone outside the total separationist movement. He indicted the NAE, Youth for Christ, International Child Evangelism Fellowship, plus allied seminaries and Bible schools as contributing to the

[3] McIntire, Modern Tower of Babel (Collingswood, N. J.: Christian Beacon Press, 1949); the NAE criticism is found in many issues of its periodical, United Evangelical Action for 1948 and 1949; see also Gasper, The Fundamentalist Movement, p. 44; and the New York Times, Aug. 21, 1948, p. 1.

spread of religious liberalism and socialism and near-communism. Under his leadership the American Council established head-quarters in New York City to propagate the faith of the earnest contenders. Most of the council programs centered on publishing pamphlets, tracts, books, tapes and distributing the many resolutions passed by the council at its meetings.

While some groups originally affiliated with the ACCC have resigned, the membership records of 1950, 1957, and 1964 show the permanent members to that date:

Bible Presbyterian Church Association;
Bible Protestant Church;
Congregational Methodist Church;
Evangelical Methodist Church of America;
General Association of Regular Baptist Churches;
Independent Churches, Affiliated;
Methodist Protestant Church;
Militant Fundamental Bible Churches;
Southern Methodist Church;
Tioga River Christian Conference;
United Christian Church;
Fundamental Methodist Church;
World Baptist Fellowship;
Independent Baptist Bible Mission.

The International Council is organized along less formal lines. It meets triennially for speeches and resolutions. It publishes a quarterly journal, *The Reformation Review,* tracts, and pamphlets. Its permanent staff has been concerned primarily with promoting separation from the World Council of Churches and with administering relief programs. Its directors refuse to publish its budget and individual membership statistics for public use.[4]

By the mid 1950's, McIntire and his two councils were best

---

[4] *Christian Beacon,* Nov. 5, 1964, p. 8; J. Oliver Buswell, Jr., "The American and International Councils of Christian Churches," *Christianity Today,* Jan. 29, 1965, pp. 9-11; some ACCC groups are described in *Handbook of Denominations in the United States,* ed. Frank S. Mead (Nashville, Abingdon Press, 1961 and later editions); for more information on the ICCC see its journal, *The Reformation Review* XIII (Oct., 1965), *passim;* by 1965 it numbered 111 members; John A. Stroman, "The American Council of Christian Churches," (Ph.D. diss., Boston University, 1966), pp. 106-32.

known in church circles for their incessant, vituperative criticisms of all nonseparationists. While the ultrafundamentalists considered this "contending earnestly for the faith," the response by the president of Princeton Theological Seminary was characteristic of those attacked: "While being concerned about Communism it carries on work with Communist technique. . . . They act without the slightest interest in truth and with terms of a Jesuitical ethic." [5] When Billy Graham refused their request to be his sole sponsor for a New York City revival, the ACCC leaders labeled his evangelism as "a victory for modernism and apostasy." In another pamphlet McIntire accused Graham of being willing to coexist with communism.[6]

Criticisms of the separationist leaders cropped up within the movement itself. In 1954, several ACCC individuals stated McIntire's administration was guilty of "undemocratic organization, hyperbolic exaggeration of statistics, and erratic leadership." [7] This apparently had grown out of an angry internal dispute over the direction of the two ACCC colleges, Highland and Shelton. When McIntire refused any concessions to the critics, a majority of delegates at the 1956 General Assembly of the Bible Presbyterian Church, which he had founded, voted to disassociate from the ACCC and his leadership. No stronger criticism of his policies could have been made. He immediately counterpunched by forming the "Bible Presbyterian Church Association" which rejoined the ACCC. No dissent was heard from those remaining with the Collingswood minister.[8]

[5] Quoted by Ralph Lord Roy, *Apostles of Discord*, p. 195; for other critical comments see Stroman, "The American Council of Christian Churches," pp. 218-25; *The Christian Century*, Sept. 14, 1949, p. 1082; Jan. 26, 1955, p. 116; and Feb. 29, 1956, pp. 260, 285-86.

[6] McIntire, et al., "A Ministry of Disobedience," a Christian Beacon pamphlet (n.d.), pp. 38-39; see Graham's response in John Pollock, *Billy Graham: The Authorized Biography* (New York: McGraw-Hill, 1966), pp. 173-74; William G. McLoughlin, *Billy Graham, Revivalist in a Secular Age* (New York: Ronald Press, 1960), pp. 226-27; ACCC Literature Item no. 120.

[7] Charges made by J. Oliver Buswell, Jr., who had stood with McIntire and Machen through the controversies of the 1930's; see his article, "The American and International Councils," *Christianity Today*, Jan. 29, 1965, pp. 9-11; Gasper, *The Fundamentalist Movement*, pp. 34-37; Stroman, "The American Council of Christian Churches," pp. 107-8.

[8] See a mimeographed study by Donald J. MacNair of Covenant College, St. Louis, Mo., entitled "Documentation Regarding the Division of the Bible Presbyterian Church"; Gasper, *The Fundamentalist Movement*, pp. 34-37, uses

In surveying the full sweep of ultrafundamentalist activity in the 1950's, the editors of *Christianity Today*, voice of the new evangelicalism, made clear what had happened:

> Carl McIntire, founder and leader of the ACCC, identified the movement with vitriolic denunciations of the inclusivist movements and churchmen, but at the same time negelcted to foster the positive tasks of evangelical thought and life. *The Christian Beacon* was not simply an ACCC house organ; it became a religious smear sheet in the worst tradition of yellow journalism.[9]

Sometime later, McIntire replied by stating that the editor of *Christianity Today*, Carl F. H. Henry, had shown "a soft hand in dealing with Communism."[10]

In summation, by late 1957, the goal McIntire had set in 1936 for separationists had been reached; those who supported him without question had separated from everyone else. With but few exceptions their program had attracted no appreciable attention within American church life. Then, rather abruptly after 1957, the ACCC–ICCC would find itself thrust into national prominence. This rapid change can best be understood by reviewing the emergence since 1945 of the second major stream of the far right, the political ideology of that movement. No attempt will be made here to present another history of American-Soviet relations. Instead, the narrative is limited to a discussion of those forces which contributed directly to the apperance of the politics of doomsday.

The cardinal doctrine of the radical right ideology is the internal conspiracy thesis; upon it all subsequent themes are constructed. Conspiratorial interpretations of America's history, however, are as old as the republic itself. Their rise in popularity

---

primary sources; the *Christian Beacon* presents its interpretation in the issues of July 12, 1956, pp. 1, 8; July 16, 1959, pp. 2, 4, 5; April 8, 1965, p. 8; Carl McIntire, *Death of a Church*, pp. 166-67; Stroman, "The American Council of Christian Churches," pp. 107-8.

[9] An editorial in the Jan. 20, 1958 issue, p. 23; Roy, *Apostles of Discord*, pp. 224-27.

[10] *Christian Beacon*, May 3, 1962, p. 3.

can usually be traced to the unexpected appearance of some alleged sinister force seeking to thwart the aspirations of the people.[11]

This general pattern reappeared shortly after V-J Day. The apparent failure of America to prevent Soviet expansion and espionage here and abroad was judged by some citizens to be the result of deliberate treasonous activity at the highest levels of their government. That conclusion rested on the belief that the course of events during and after World War II spoke for itself. Had not almost every American believed that his nation had rescued Europe and the world from the hideous reign of the Nazis? Had not almost every citizen believed that the Soviet Union could not conceivably want to risk further destruction by war after having so recently suffered such fearful losses of life and property? Had not almost every American believed that so long as his government maintained complete control over nuclear weapons the world would never again be faced with the threat of nuclear warfare? Could it be doubted that America's participation in the war was the will of God; that in his love he chose the nation most closely embodying the ideals of Christianity to destroy Satan's lieutenants? Considering all this, no man of good will could deny this blessed nation had been ordained to establish and protect man's noble dreams of peace and justice.

Proponents of the internal conspiracy thesis added the historical record to support their rhetoric. The dreams for a *Pax Americanus* had been demonically destroyed by the Communists; they had taken over the Balkan and Baltic nations; they had disrupted the UN with the veto; they had refused to work with the West in the Marshall Plan and Point Four; their aggression had forced the Allies into the Berlin Airlift and the creation of NATO. Above all, in 1949 they had achieved nuclear parity. One year later Stalin had ordered the Communist invasion of South Korea. Suddenly the United States had lost the initiative; communism, not liberty, was advancing around the globe.

Some hard questions had to be answered: Since America

[11] See, for example, the first essay of Richard Hofstadter, *The Paranoid Style in American Politics and Others Essays* (New York: Alfred A. Knopf, 1965), and Arthur M. Schlesinger, Sr., "Extremism in American Politics," *Saturday Review*, Nov. 27, 1965, pp. 21-25.

had not chosen war, hot or cold, why were only Amreican but not Russian troops dying in combat? Why was the world's most powerful arsenal so quickly dismantled? Why was America still trying to negotiate through traditional channels with the Soviet Union? Why had China fallen so quickly to the Communists?

Most Americans were asking these questions, but not all of them traced the results exclusively to the internal conspiracy. That was the conclusion, however, of a small but vocal number of citizens. They refused to believe that this takeover was the work of skillful imperialists within the Kremlin. Rather, they decided that most if not all American foreign policy making had been dominated for several years by highly skillful Soviet espionage agents and their willing dupes working within this nation. So successful had these subversives become in establishing themselves in the centers of power that most Americans had all but overlooked even the possibility that such a conspiracy could exist.

The climate of opinion which had inspired such infamy, the argument stated, could be traced back to the beginnings of the New Deal of 1933, when the large number of experimental reform measures enacted then to combat the Depression attracted many socialists and Communists to Washington. This tampering created an atmosphere of pragmatism, flexibility, and indifference toward the traditional governmental duty of protecting the historic ideals of individualism, self-discipline, free enterprise, and isolation from global involvement. Since these qualities were expressions of a divinely inspired natural law, universally true for all men, then it must follow that the deviations since 1933 would explain accurately the failure of America to recognize what the liberals-socialists-Communists had accomplished within its government. Only one firm conclusion was possible; traitors and dupes had conspired to sell out America to communism.

Into this milieu stepped the junior senator of Wisconsin. Joseph R. McCarthy did not claim to invent anticommunism. He did not expose any Communists, fellow travelers, pinkos, or dupes not already known to the authorized investigative agencies in Washington. His activities, however, would create a broad legacy which contributed greatly to the shaping of the far right movement of the 1960's. Rather than attempt a summary of his career, this writer will suggest several of his contributions to anticommunism which would be used by the radical right.[12]

During the four years of the senator's greatest influence, 1950-54, most of the basic ideology of the far right took shape. Although its themes had been publicized before 1950, they needed and finally received the official sanction of as high an offical as a United State senator. His prestige and skillful use of the mass media promoted the doctrines of the far right in every section of the country.

Those who accepted the conspiracy thesis found it suddenly unlocked the mysterious doors of the never-never land of official Washington, "The Establishment." Once the believer in conspiracy understood its ramifications, he could see where it was leading America and what he could do to save his nation. He learned the meaning of liberalism, too, and it was not the harmless planning of ivory tower utopians. No, liberalism was tantamount to socialism because both systems relied on collective rather than individual solutions. Once a society had sold out to liberalism it had taken an irrevocable step toward socialism, and that system was but one step removed from communism. It could not be any other way. Communism was totally evil since its foundations were atheistic and materialistic. Thus, those who accepted liberalism were embracing atheism; only conservatives were loyal to Christ.

The great contest in the world was not simply communism versus capitalism; it was good fighting evil. America could win that battle only if she purged herself immediately of those insidious forces within which were destroying her will to fight back. If America would only see that her greatest and most trustworthy source of strength was her Christian heritage. God could not fail, but America was failing God. The Puritans and the constitutional fathers had established a republic based on divinely inspired laws to guarantee the full expression of individual freedom. Those laws, more than similar laws of any other nation, were reflections of his will for man. Knowing this, the Christian American sees that God intends nothing less for his most beloved nation than total victory over collectivism—call it liberalism, socialism, or communism—

[12] The differences between the McCarthy crusade and the far right are discussed later, pp. 65-67.

wherever it existed. The world would not be free until those forces of evil have been physically destroyed.[13]

This ideology came into prominence in the early 1950's. A decade later the radical right repeated the same themes with equal vigor.

A second area of common ground between McCarthyites and far rightists is of special importance for the rise of ultrafundamentalism. Both groups believed the American Protestant clergy was deeply pockmarked with Communists and their willing sympathizers. Much of the documentation on this subject was carried from the Wisconsin senator to the far right by J. B. Matthews. In 1952, he endeared himself to the budding anti-Communist movement by stating that some seven thousand Protestant clergymen in America served communism. That charge, in the form of an article for *American Mercury*, later became a best seller in the world of McIntire, Hargis, Bundy, and Kaub.[14]

Finally, with his many-sided program of investigation, Senator McCarthy established unity and gave momentum to the feelings of those citizens who no longer believed their elected public officials could cope with the internal conspiracy. Such a wholesale decline in trust was quite without precedent in American history. It would become a major characteristic of the radical right.

In summary, while the Wisconsin lawmaker became the most popular leader among the proponents of the conspiracy thesis, he consciously stopped short of establishing a fully organized movement. That task would be carried out shortly after his death primarily by two unlikely candidates; a Boston candymaker and a New Jersey ecclesiologist. To understand the reasons for the merger of the religious and political streams of fundamentalism of the far right, it is necessary to trace briefly the response made by the ultrafundamentalists to the direction of world events.

[13] See McCarthy, *McCarthyism: The Fight for America* (New York: Devin-Adair, 1952); McCarthy, *Major Speeches and Debates of Senator Joe McCarthy Delivered in the United States Senate, 1950-1951,* published privately and distributed by the Bookmailer, Inc.; Michael Paul Rogin, *The Intellectuals and McCarthy: The Radical Specter* (Cambridge: Massachusetts Institute of Technology Press, 1967), chaps. 8-9.

[14] *Christian Beacon,* Sept. 15, 1955, p. 8; Matthew's portrait in oil hangs alongside McIntire's in the Christian Admiral Hotel, summer headquarters of the Twentieth Century Reformation. For additional discussion of Matthews, see pp. 55-56.

The first extended discussion of ultrafundamentalist political thought appeared in 1944, when McIntire published a full length study, *Twentieth Century Reformation*. He brought out a revised edition the next year along with a second work, *The Rise of the Tyrant: Controlled Economy vs. Private Enterprise*. A third volume of his, *Author of Liberty*, appeared in 1946, the same year Verne P. Kaub made his first important contribution, a full length work entitled *Collectivism Challenges Christianity*.[15]

Both authors made the same point: "We do not want modernism, pacifism, near-communism! Do we? We want America free, as God's Word demands." By promoting Christianity, "Free Government," "Free Enterprise," and "The American Way," the nation's citizens had created the most ideal conditions ever known for advancing God's Word.[16]

In 1945, McIntire went on to insist that America faced a mortal threat not only from communism, but from "a pagan, false religion that enslaves and damns the souls of men." The New Jersey clergyman applied this insight to world politics.

As we enter the postwar world, without any doubt the greatest enemy of freedom and liberty that the world has to face today is the Roman Catholic system. Yes, we have Communism in Russia and all that is involved there, but if one had to choose between the two . . . one would be much better off in a Communistic society, than in a Roman Catholic fascist setup. One wonders sometimes if all the antagonism of the Roman Catholic Church to Communism . . . is not being played up especially to the United States at the present time for the purpose of gaining advantage for the Roman Catholics. . . . America has to face the Roman Catholic terror. The sooner the Christian people of America wake up to this danger, the safer will be our land.[17]

---

[15] The Christian Beacon Press publishes McIntire's books. The edition used here of *Collectivism Challenges Christianity* is the 1961 paperback issued by the American Council of Christian Laymen.

[16] McIntire, *Twentieth Century Reformation*, p. 217; Kaub, *Collectivism*, pp. 1, 54; in his "Introduction," Kaub acknowledges how closely his book parallels McIntire's *The Rise of the Tyrant*; see *Collectivism*, pp. xxx-xxxi.

[17] *Christian Beacon*, Sept. 6, 1945, pp. 1, 8, Stroman, "The American Council of Christian Churches," p. 125-27; Roy, *Apostles of Discord*, pp. 165-68.

As the cold war intensified in the late 1940's, McIntire spotted the spread of the internal conspiracy into Protestant circles. He detected treason in the World Council of Churches, the nation's nonseparated seminaries and colleges, and even in some Bible schools. He explained that "a master plan and a master mind is behind these thrusts." However he withheld the name of the master mind.[18]

Perhaps the most memorable solution proposed by the ACCC to Communist penetration at home and abroad was published in 1948, before the world knew the Soviets had nuclear weapons. The relevant passages read:

> We call upon the representatives of freedom-loving nations for a complete and frank showdown with Russia. The longer we delay, as the last three years has indicated, the more complicated the situation develops and the more disillusioned and despairing the forces for morality become. For us to have the atom bomb, and in the name of a false morality, born of a perverted sense of self-respect and pacifist propaganda, to await the hour when Russia has her bombs to precipitate an atomic war, is the height of insanity and will, when the fateful hour comes, be a just punishment upon us.
>
> We believe that Almighty God holds us responsible.[19]

Several months later the executive board of the American Council of Christian Churches, the official policy making body, called for war. Convinced the Soviets were preparing to attack the United States, the members declared that America had "a moral responsibility to strike first using adequate and necessary ways to thwart the maddened purpose of the enemy." [20]

Clearly, the ultrafundamentalists were constructing a political ideology on the foundations of their theology. Verbal inerrancy informed them that only they understood God's word for this age. Separationism taught them only they were pure enough to fight the satanic triad of liberalism-socialism-communism. Apocalyptic premillennialism assured them that their call for war

[18] *Christian Beacon*, Sept. 9, 1948, p. 8; Sept. 23, 1948, pp. 1, 8.
[19] *Christian Beacon*, Nov. 4, 1948, p. 2.
[20] A news item issued by Religious News Service, as quoted in Stroman, "The American Council of Christian Churches," pp. 193-94.

50

with Russia was not really warmongering; since only God could destroy this planet and since that would not happen until after the Final Judgment, Americans need not fear any form of nuclear warfare. These three doctrines, as applied to world events in the early 1950's, would become a decade later the essence of the politics of doomsday.

Two events in 1950 gave the ultrafundamentalists the opportunity to expand the national scope of the "Twentieth Century Reformation." To strengthen programs of mutual interest, twelve interdenominational church service agencies, the largest being the Federal Council of Churches, combined with twenty-nine denominations to create the National Council of Churches of Christ in the U.S.A. Here, to McIntire, was final proof of the fulfillment of Scriptural prophecy. Now, the "superchurch," the Whore of Babylon foretold in Revelation, was making itself known. The Antichrist in the name of "social Christianity" was reaching out to clutch the world into his grasp. The true believer should rejoice because the appearance of the NCC proved God was bringing this corrupt world to an end. He would not allow Christians to suffer such evil much longer.[21]

To win over any doubters, McIntire offered proof for his charge. He joined forces for the first time with Verne Kaub who had just founded the American Council of Christian Laymen. Already known for his *Collectivism Challenges Christianity*, Kaub collaborated with McIntire in publishing a tract, "How Red is the National [printed over the word 'Federal'] Council of Churches?" Most of the research had been done by J. B. Matthews. To them the NCC was apostate, un-American, pro-Communist, and treasonous. The authors pleaded:

Don't give it one dollar. The National Council receives large sums from various Jewish and other non-Christian or anti-Christian groups, so while the withdrawal of your church's support won't put them out of business, it will hurt them.[22]

---

[21] This theme was developed by McIntire in most issues of the *Christian Beacon* for 1950 and 1951, and in several Twentieth Century Reformation tracts.

[22] See note 28 of this chapter for more information on Matthews; Roy, *Apostles of Discord*, pp. 244-50; Gasper, *The Fundamentalist Movement*, pp. 64-69; Paul Hutchinson, "The J. B. Matthews Story," *The Christian Century*, July 29, 1953, pp. 864-66.

The authors failed to identify the "non-" and "anti-Christian" groups. The charges and the tone of "How Red. . . ?" harmonized perfectly with the outlook of the ACCC–ICCC. The pamphlet quickly became and remains a basic staple in all ultrafundamentalist enterprises.

The work of McIntire, Kaub, and other fledgling far rightists would perhaps have gone unnoticed had not the second decisive event of 1950 appeared at just this time. In February, Senator Joseph McCarthy gave in Wheeling, West Virginia, the first of what would be hundreds of freewheeling attacks on "Reds" in the American government. The ultrafundamentalists realized suddenly they had found the national leader they needed. They responded quickly. Billy James Hargis, then an obscure revivalist in Oklahoma, came to Washington where, in his words, "I wrote the famous speech about G. Bromley Oxnam that Senator McCarthy delivered on the Senate floor." Later, in discussing his investigations, the senator stated he had received help "from a great preacher, Dr. Billy James Hargis of Tulsa, Oklahoma, who is pastor of a church there and is doing outstanding work. Some of the information also came from the International Council of Christian Churches." McCarthy added that the ICCC was a "militant anti-Communist group" whose ministers were "usefully serving the interests of America and God." [23] It is not known whether McCarthy, himself a Roman Catholic, knew Dr. McIntire, president of the ICCC, had characterized the Roman Catholic Church as one that enslaved and damned the souls of men.

True to their conviction, born in 1938, that America's worst internal enemies were her clergymen, the ultrafundamentalists thrust themselves into the McCarthyite offensive. Their enthusiasm for exposing "Reds in the Churches" endeared them to those elected officials eager to have the job done but less than en-

[23] The quote by Hargis is in Pete Martin, "I Call on Billy James Hargis," *Christian Herald*, March, 1967, p. 70; the speech Hargis refers to was not printed in the permanent bound edition of the *Congressional Record*. In a letter to me of April 14, 1967, Hargis wrote he had typed the speech in Washington and believed McCarthy had it deleted from the *Congressional Record* just before he died. In another place Hargis stated that the senator was the first celebrity to give Christian Crusade "a national boost"; *Christian Crusade*, Nov., 1965, p. 33; the remarks on the ICCC by McCarthy are found in the newspaper of Harvey Springer, *Western Voice*, Feb. 29, 1956, pp. 1, 3; Springer was a close associate of McIntire.

thusiastic about doing it themselves for fear of voter disapproval. This tacit alliance explains why for the next five years the ACCC-ICCC leaders found themselves sought out by broadcasters and reporters who knew a good front-page story in the making—Communists among the clergy, the Revised Standard Version of the Bible a Red plot, the World Council of Churches a front for Soviet espionage. Of such stuff are eye-catching stories made.

This alliance also explains why several congressmen of the investigative committees drew up their charges against the allegedly treasonous clergymen, using the evidence enthusiastically furnished by the ultrafundamentalists. The lawmakers found their own probes greatly accelerated by having at their fingertips a large amount of data on the suspects. In turn, McIntire and his supporters, who had been known primarily for their flamboyant statements on Billy Graham and Roman Catholicism, were able to claim that even congressmen turned to them for their evidence in pursuing their authorized investigations. The probes, in short, helped give the ultrafundamentalists the kind of respectability their programs so badly needed.

From early 1950 until late in 1954, the ACCC–ICCC leaders cooperated with Senator McCarthy's staff and even more directly with that of the House Un-American Activities Committee. Perhaps the best-known episodes were those in which the ultrafundamentalists pressed for congressional investigations into the activities of two prominent Methodist ministers, Dr. E. Stanley Jones and Bishop G. Bromley Oxnam, and the translation of the Revised Standard Version of the Bible.

McIntire had been pursuing Jones as early as 1944, labeling him then "a bishop of near-Communism . . . a missionary for a communistic new social order." [24] In 1950, Jones was touring the nation speaking for the adoption of the proposed National Council of Churches, which to McIntire was the tool of Satan. No congressional committee took up the suggestion that Jones be investigated. However McIntire did receive publicity over the issue. The matter also produced an exchange of letters between himself and Jones which are near-classic in their delineation of the issues at stake, and are quoted here at length for that reason.

[24] McIntire, *Twentieth Century Reformation*, p. 168.

53

On Good Friday, April 7, 1950, Jones wrote to McIntire:

Today we both stand before the judgment of the Cross. I pray that all that is in me that is unlike that Man, who hung on the Cross to redeem us with His own blood, may be taken out of me.

On April 10 McIntire replied:

I do not believe, Dr. Jones, that I now stand before the judgment of the cross. Christ endured once and for all the wrath of God in judgment for me. I am freed from it all by His precious death. . . .

On April 24 Jones wrote:

The cross means to you redemption, but there is no further judgment there for you. I agree with you that the cross is redemption, but I believe that the cross judges everything in me not in conformity with the spirit of the Man who hung on that cross for me. So the cross sends me into the highest heaven of joy for the release from myself and my sins and at that very moment sends me to my knees in judgment upon all that still does not completely conform to that spirit manifested on that cross. So at once it exalts me and humbles me. You say it exalts you but does not humble you—does not judge you. In other words you feel that there is nothing in you that is not in harmony with the spirit of the Man who hung there. Your continued redemption is sterilized by your viewpoint. You end in self-righteousness. . . . Not being judged by the cross you then proceed to set up a judgment seat of your own . . . that makes you hard, censorious, critical. The pay-off is in you. You become what you give out. You become a critical person.[25]

Unquestionably the most spectacular attempt by McIntire to use congressional investigators for earnest contending burst

[25] The April 7 and April 10 letters are in the *Christian Beacon*, April 13, 1950, p. 1; the April 24 letter is in the May 4, 1950, issue, p. 2; they are also found in Stroman, "The American Council of Christian Churches," Appendix VII, pp. 302-4. I have deleted a few sentences from the conclusion of the second Jones letter.

into the press in 1952, when the ACCC–ICCC found Communist conspiracies at work in the Revised Standard Version of the Bible. For a few days McIntire's name remained on page one of the nation's newspapers with his charge that the RSV was "an unholy book . . . the work of Satan and his agents." [26] Some conservative Protestant scholars had found certain translations unacceptable, but it was McIntire who found the RSV both un-American and Communistic. With the very Word of God now under attack, he asked, could the last days be far off? [27]

The year 1953 produced the best opportunity yet for the ultrafundamentalists to influence the workings of congressional investigations. Senator McCarthy found a series of eye-catching articles in the *American Mercury,* especially in the July issue, exposing "Reds in our Churches." The author was J. B. Matthews, already well established with Kaub and McIntire for his work on "How Red. . . ?" The Wisconsinite apparently was prepared to accept Matthews' indictment of the ministers:

> The largest single group supporting the Communist apparatus in the United States today is composed of Protestant clergymen. The Communist party has enlisted the support of at least seven thousand Protestant clergymen [as] party The largest single group supporting the Communist apherents, and unwitting dupes.[28]

Matthews was appointed executive director of the McCarthy investigative operation for the Senate. Once the charges he had made against the clergy were made public, fellow senators, American ministers, and laity protested immediately and furiously, demanding Matthews' removal. President Eisenhower denounced the "generalized and irresponsible attacks that sweepingly con-

[26] *Denver Post,* Dec. 10, 1952, p. 29.
[27] See the *Christian Beacon* for October and November, 1952, especially Oct. 23 and Oct. 30, *passim;* the NCC replied in several pamphlets, the most complete being "An Open Letter Concerning the Revised Standard Version of the Bible"; he also objected to the fact that the NCC owned the copyright on the new translation. The NCC had done this to preserve the integrity of the text against pirateering.
[28] See the *American Mercury* LXXVII July, 1953, 3-13; reprints today are always available from any ultrafundamentalist office.

demn the whole of any group." So intense was the criticism that seventeen days after the appointment, Senator McCarthy announced Matthews' resignation. Throughout the uproar, McIntire and his supporters stoutly defended Matthews and gave full endorsement to his articles in the *American Mercury*.[29] As will be discussed later, Matthews went on to become a full-time researcher for several far right organizations.

This setback failed to dampen McIntire's zest for the action in Washington. As was disclosed later, the ACCC in 1953 furnished the House Un-American Activities Committee with considerable information alleging that Bishop G. Bromley Oxnam was a "top Red clergyman" in America. An outspoken advocate of the church's social responsibilities, a vigorous proponent of ecumenical cooperation, and a pungent critic of the work of Senator McCarthy and HUAC, Oxnam had come to personify the ideals McIntire found obnoxious in American church life.

The ACCC mounted a full offensive for a congressional investigation. Here would be prize exhibit number one of what they had been telling the public all the time. After a long series of rallies, petitions, tracts, sermons, and general hullabaloo, the ACCC requested a full probe by the House. Oxnam himself surprised everyone by volunteering to meet before HUAC under oath to answer all charges. On July 21 the meeting was held. Oxnam tried to get into the record the fact that much of the evidence against him in the files of the committee had been given by the ACCC, but the chairman ruled him out of order. For ten hours the congressmen and the bishop went over his past activities. At the conclusion the members voted unanimously that they had found no evidence to indicate Oxnam had belonged to the Communist party.[30]

Public interest in "Red clergy" declined quickly after the Oxnam hearings, and the ultrafundamentalists could not restore

[29] *New York Times,* see p. 1 for July 3, 4, 7, 8, 1953 and p. 11 for July 7, 1953; Ralph Lord Roy, *Communism and the Churches* (New York: Harcourt, Brace, 1960), pp. 248-53; Hutchinson, "The J. B. Matthews Story," *The Christian Century,* July 29, 1953, pp. 864-66.

[30] Gasper, *The Fundamentalist Movement,* pp. 64-69; *The Christian Century,* Nov. 4, 1953, p. 1273; Aug. 5, 1953, p. 885; *New York Times,* July 22, 1953, p. 4; McIntire's views on Oxnam are summarized in his *Modern Tower of Babel,* chap. 12.

reader interest in the ensuing months. However, the episode helped the ACCC–ICCC in one crucial area; a substantial amount of new revenue came into McIntire's office. This allowed the leaders to expand their operations in several directions. An early step was the hiring of two new workers, Billy James Hargis and Fred C. Schwarz.

To demonstrate their loyalty to the earlier, nonrevised version of the Bible, the ACCC–ICCC leaders under McIntire's direction employed Hargis to supervise their "Bible Balloon Project." On the German-Czechoslovakian border, in 1953, he and several helpers placed portions of Scripture, translated into several Slavic languages, in helium-filled balloons and floated these into Iron Curtain nations. While the impact of the program was difficult to assess, the event did produce international publicity for Hargis and brought him directly into the realm of the Twentieth Century Reformation for the first time.

Dr. Schwarz associated himself with the American and International Councils during the same year. He made a speaking tour of several of the councils' congregations. McIntire and other officials were satisfied enough with his tour to encourage him to stay in America. Schwarz accepted the invitation and made this event the formal beginning of his anticommunism crusade in the United States.[81]

By the end of 1953, then, the men who would come to be recognized as the leaders of fundamentalism of the far right were all actively working for or directly with the ACCC–ICCC. McIntire was the acknowledged executive, Bundy was his closest associate, Hargis was on the payroll, and Kaub and Matthews were furnishing the kind of documentation the spokesmen wanted.

With their crusades well under way, the ultrafundamentalists and McCarthyites had every reason to believe 1954 would be even better than the boom of 1953. In their enthusiasm, however, they would mistake the zeal of their supporters for that of wide general approval. For McCarthy the error would be fatal. The story of the "Army-McCarthy" hearings is too well known to bear repeating here. As the confrontation was televised across the nation the public support on which the senator so strongly depended

[81] Discussed in more detail on p. 69.

slowly slipped away. The Senate itself in December voted 67 to 22 to censure McCarthy for certain activities and statements.

The American Council soon found itself in a similar dilemma. It had decided to wage an all-out barrage on the Assembly of the World Council of Churches, scheduled for Evanston, Illinois, in August. Realizing they could not stop the delegates from convening, the leaders decided to work for a smaller but potentially newsworthy goal—persuading the State Department to refuse entry visas to four officials labeled by the ACCC as "Communist clergy." The four named were the General Secretary of the WCC, W. A. Visser 't Hooft, Bishops Berezky and Arvidson, and Professor Joseph Hromadka. By exposing the fact that these men were at Evanston, the ACCC hoped to prove how serious a threat the World Council was to Christianity and America.

Edgar C. Bundy took the first step in the 1954 program. He convinced the Cook County, Illinois, American Legion to pass a resolution calling on the State Department to prohibit the entrance of these men into America. While some Chicago Legionaires gave it their full support, other influential shapers of public opinion found the resolution unacceptable. It was criticized by the staunchly conservative *Chicago Tribune* on the editorial pages. Col. Robert McCormick's staff stated the resolution was "no credit to Chicago" and welcomed delegates from Iron Curtain nations with the suggestion they compare their own nation's life to that of America.

McIntire countered by printing the Cook County resolution in the *Christian Beacon* and asked his readers to pass it on to their local Legionaires. The Bundy resolution came before the national executive committee of the American Legion in May. After a brief debate it was turned down. At the World Council Assembly itself, the ACCC–ICCC demonstrated with rallies, pickets, placards, and pamphlets. The four accused clergymen attended the meetings.[32]

The Senate censure and the failure to accomplish anything at Evanston signified declining public support for McCarthy and the ultrafundamentalists. At the same time, world events con-

[32] Gasper, *The Fundamentalist Movement*, pp. 69-71; *The Christian Century*, March 24, 1954, p. 356; April 28, 1954, pp. 507-08; May 5, 1954, p. 550; May 19, 1954, p. 603.

tributed to a new spirit in foreign affairs. The death of Stalin, the more moderate tone toward America by the new Soviet leaders, and the end of the stalemate in Korea all helped deflate some of the hard line anticommunism of the early 50's. What the Mc-Carthyites and ultrafundamentalists needed was the kind of leadership they had known in their heyday. Senator McCarthy, however, failed to reassert his command after the rebuke by the Senate, and none of his close associates picked up his sceptre after his death in 1957. The momentum had slowed to a creep; the old spark was lost.

3
Unity and Diversity, 1958-61

By 1958, followers of Senator McCarthy found themselves facing a crisis. They believed American strength at home and abroad was declining at a terrifying rate, yet the public was ignoring the growing internal conspiracy and was even ridiculing those who were carrying on their departed leader's cause. Since his labors must not be wasted, someone must rise up now with a program to save America. It was not too late; the public could be made to understand the perilous future if it only had all the information, if it could be taught that liberalism (be it Democratic or Republican) was carrying this nation down the road to Moscow. America needed a leader; it needed many leaders who could revive the Christian heritage of free enterprise and liberty. Senator McCarthy could not have been expected to have accomplished all that. He had taken the first step, he had exposed the subversives. Now the enemy must be rooted out of every dark corner of America.

Somewhere between 1958 and 1961, with the inauguration of John F. Kennedy as president, the radical right was born. Somewhere in that time the religious and political streams of separationism and nationalism merged to become fundamentalism of the far right. Obviously no one cut a ribbon or sponsored a grand-opening merger party announcing that the crusade was now open for business and gratefully accepting contributions. But the fresh burst of energy expressed by old McCarthyites, ultra-fundamentalists, and recent converts signified the beginnings of a new assault on the internal conspiracy.

Nothing could be done without money, and somewhere the ultrafundamentalists as well as far rightists found the means to fill their waiting treasuries. The table below needs only a brief explanation.[1] Almost all the contributions made to the ultra-fundamentalist programs came in small quantities; hence the growth rate indicated that in the late 1950's an increasing number of citizens were giving. Second, the figures of the table represent thousands of dollars. Finally, the last three organizations listed here obviously were not in the ACCC–ICCC but have been included for purposes of comparison. The figures for Kaub's American Council of Christian Laymen are not available.

Most of this material was collected by Group Research, Inc. and published in September, 1964.

	1955	1956	1957	1958	1959	1960
Twentieth Century Reformation	25.8	25.0	38.5	62.0	177.5	382.5
Christian Crusade	48.4	124.1	170.7	275.3	373.2	595.5
Church League of America	21.8	29.4	38.9	49.9	50.2	78.2
Human Events	151.6	237.9	301.9	329.1	390.4	594.6
Americans for Constitutional Action	(not in existence)			5.7	197.7	126.8
John Birch Society	(not in existence)				129.8	198.7

A second symptom of the new movement was the formal constituting of the John Birch Society in 1958. Its birth was kept a secret for two years, but the fact that it did appear suggested a new outlook and new need among hard-line ultraconservatives. McCarthy was gone; no one had replaced him. Perhaps, as Robert Welch suggested, it was time for rebuilding from the bottom up.[2]

A third symptom was the fact that by the late 1950's the

[1] Based on figures from "The Finances of the Far Right," Special Report no. 16, Sept. 1, 1964 (Group Research, Inc.: Washington, D. C.), passim.

[2] See his account in any early edition of The Blue Book (Belmont, Mass.); also J. Allen Broyles, The John Birch Society: Anatomy of a Protest (Boston: Beacon Press, 1964), chaps. 1-2.

objections of militant conservatives to the administration of President Dwight D. Eisenhower had been hardened into implacable opposition. Nothing could be more clear to a potential far rightist than the fact that the president's policies were giving aid and comfort to the Communists. The record again spoke for itself; the internal conspiracy was once again at work. It appeared in many beguiling forms: foreign aid to nations "where atheism is sponsored and promoted"; peaceful coexistence rather than a total victory policy; payment of the debts of the United Nations, an organization destroying American sovereignty and turning its citizens into Communists; permission for clergymen from Iron Curtain nations to visit this country; recognition by the president and the Secretary of State, John Foster Dulles, of the National and World Councils of Churches, both of which were pawns in Moscow's game; failure to recognize creeping Castroism in the Caribbean, refusal to send arms to the Hungarian rebels. Unless the trend was immediately and permanently checked, America would fall to communism.[3]

The record was equally bad at home. The president had ordered federal troops to invade the sovereign state of Arkansas and disrupt its constitutional right to regulate public education. The federal budget was growing, not declining. The Communist party in America was expanding. Nothing had been done to reverse the "pro-Red" decisions of the Supreme Court. And the future seemed even more bleak. By 1958, no sound conservative had appeared within the Republican party to challenge the claims of Richard Nixon, the choice of the eastern liberals, to the throne in 1960.

[3] A Christian Crusade tract, "This I Believe," p. 5 (all Crusade tracts and pamphlets are undated); W. Cleon Skousen, *The Naked Communist*, 9th ed. (Salt Lake City: Ensign Publishing Company, 1961), pp. 223-88; Roy, *Communism and the Churches*, pp. 229-30; Edgar C. Bundy, *Collectivism in the Churches* (Wheaton, Ill.: The Church League of America, 1960), chaps. 5-16; Bundy, *How the Communists Use Religion* (New York: Devin-Adair, 1966), *passim; News and Views,* July, 1962 (the organ of the CLA); Ralph E. Ellsworth and Sarah M. Harris, *The American Right Wing: A Report to the Fund for the Republic* (Washington: Public Affairs Press, 1962), pp. 41-45; McIntire, *Modern Tower of Babel*, pp. 36, 179, 260; McIntire, *Servants of Apostasy*, p. 164 and chaps. 10-11; Arnold Forster and Benjamin R. Epstein, *Danger on the Right* (New York: Random House, 1964), p. 107; Gasper, *The Fundamentalist Movement*, pp. 46-54.

The conclusion was inescapable. America now must recognize that she was at war; the enemy was everywhere, the conspiracy was growing more deadly each day. Only a massive program of exposing the liberals and of rededication to the ideals of Americanism could preserve this nation.[4]

The budding far rightist also could point to hard facts indicating the spread of the internal conspiracy into every corner of national life. In the late 1950's, it seemed as though moral laxness was spreading rapidly through local governmental agencies, such as the corruptness in the Denver and Chicago police forces. Price fixing among the giant electrical corporations revealed a breakdown in standards there. Added to that was the increasing crime rate and the easier access to pornographic materials and illegal narcotics. This was only additional proof in far rightist thinking that American life had entered a dizzy, downward spiral from its once stern Puritan morality. These developments did not just happen; someone was responsible for all this. Each of these developments gave aid and comfort to communism because each weakened America.[5]

Another portent of the new movement was the appearance of a new attitude towards the study of communism. For a decade following V-J Day, hard-line anti-Communists had attempted to suppress the study of Marx, Engels, Lenin, Stalin, and related topics in the schools. Controversial speakers or "leftists," such as Harold Laski, found lecture halls closed to them; loyalty oaths were popular; copies of The Nation and New Republic were removed from library shelves.[6]

Such hostility disappeared sometime after 1954. It is impossible to say with any certainty whether Senator McCarthy's

[4] Robert Welch, The Politician, passim; this was first published privately in the mid-1950's. The first edition available to the public came out in 1963. For the relationships between the John Birch Society and the fundamentalists of the far right see pp. 111-13.

[5] Ellsworth and Harris, The American Right Wing, pp. 43-44; Richard Hofstadter, The Paranoid Style, pp. 80-82; Robert Lee, "Social Sources of the Radical Right," The Christian Century, pp. 595-97; see the attack by Hargis on the Eisenhower administration in his book Communist America—Must It Be? chap. 2, and in his article, "A Christian Ambassador Surveys the Divided World," American Mercury LXXXV (Oct., 1957), 141-45.

[6] John W. Caughey, In Clear and Present Danger: The Crucial State of Our Freedoms (Chicago: University of Chicago Press, 1958), pp. 10-11.

decline had any direct impact on the change. But a widespread demand did appear on all educational and public levels for more information about communism. Apparently a major shift in public thinking occurred at about that time. Instead of worrying about the contamination of one's mind as a result of reading on communism, now ultraconservatives were stating that if Americans knew their enemy, they could the more easily defeat him. A whole new industry—the supply of information about communism in its many aspects—soon grew to be a multimillion dollar enterprise.

Suppliers quickly furnished low-priced, well-edited exposés of the conspiracy. They also added one vital ingredient that had been missing in earlier publications of this type. They employed "expert" advisors and speakers to supplement their programs. Almost every group had at least one ex-Communist, or former F.B.I. agent, or retired military leader to write or lecture the customers on Marxism-Leninism, Soviet foreign policy, or internal subversion.

With new resources for promotion, these groups now found means of opening new doors for their form of education. They found ready markets at corporation meetings, factory programs, civic meetings, patriotic rallies, and school convocations. The talks, films, or tapes would consist of anything from a luncheon program to a week-long "countersubversion seminar." Usually the speaker and his associataes would also offer a complete line of books, pamphlets, tapes, films, records, and other materials suitable for anti-Communist education at most age levels.

Almost every one of these enterprises was successful. The expert, complete with low-priced materials, carried the hard-line message into the towns and villages of the nation which had previously lacked access to such information. Here was material not available from what the far right called the "liberal-left press," television or radio. It was heavily illustrated, usually in four colors, and easy to understand. In this manner the widely-varied materials of the anti-Communist "think factories," such as Harding College or Bundy's Church League, were accepted as authoritative by those without previous extensive exposure to the complexities of these subjects.

The local residents now had materials to use for documentation as they debated textbooks, the PTA, the National Education

Association, or the National Council of Churches. No comparable organization or publishing firm or speaker's bureau existed to offer rebuttal to their charges. The local priest or pastor who might be moderate or liberal in politics, or the moderate-to-liberal local political leader, editor, or educator was forced to rely on his own ingenuity to produce documentation refuting the mountains of materials coming from the newly-expanded far right publishing houses. This often proved to be a difficult task.[7]

In summary, with these factors weighing in on him, the potential far rightist decided he must organize or perish. In the late 1950's, individuals from every region, every income bracket, virtually every profession, and from all major and many minor church denominations started to form into what would become known as the "radical" or "far right."

This movement, as suggested above, was in part, but only in part, the outgrowth of the anti-Communist activities of Senator Joseph R. McCarthy. The differences between his movement and that which became the "far right" were as profound as the similarities. The most obvious contrast between the two crusades was found in the opponents each attacked. The Wisconsinite concentrated almost exclusively on the issue of spies, fellow travelers, and security risks. He showed little sustained interest in other major domestic issues. He frequently voted in the "moderate" Republican bloc on welfare legislation, public housing, and social security. He rarely criticized organized labor. One staunch conservative, L. Brent Bozell, coauthor of an apologetic for the senator, stated he felt "terrible" about McCarthy's inconsistent conservatism; in Bozell's judgment the senator was "more and more like a Left liberal in domestic affairs." [8] The radical right, on

[7] See examples in Harry and Bonaro Overstreet, *The Strange Tactics of Extremism* (New York: W. W. Norton, 1964), chap. 17; Donald Janson and Bernard Eismann, *The Far Right* (New York: McGraw-Hill, 1963), chaps. 11-14; Alan F. Westin, "Anti-Communism and the Corporations," *Commentary* XXXVI (Dec., 1963), 479-87; Toch, *The Social Psychology of Social Movements*, pp. 67-68; Howard and Arlene Eisenberg, "The Far Right and the Churches," *The Progressive* XXIX (July, Aug., 1965), 15-18, 20-23; George Thayer, *The Farther Shore of Politics: The American Political Fringe* (New York: Simon and Schuster, 1967), chap. 7 and pp. 272-78.

[8] Richard H. Rovere, *Senator Joe McCarthy* (New York: Harcourt, Brace, 1959), p. 241; Seymour Martin Lipset, "Three Decades of the Radical Right: Coughlinites, McCarthyites, and Birchers," in *The Radical Right* ed. Daniel Bell

the other hand, rejected any "moderate" stance on domestic issues.

A second dissimilarity emerged over McCarthy's failure to attract the support of the several professional hate groups specializing in anti-Catholicism and anti-Semitism. Himself a Catholic and having as his most publicized aides Roy Cohn and G. David Schine, he did not receive noticeable help from the likes of Gerald L. K. Smith and others who today constitute a small but noisy faction among the far rightists.

Some support for McCarthy came from registered Democratic voters who were Catholics and supported him because of his religious beliefs. Such support was not carried into the 1960's because, as Ralph Lord Roy shows, it would be very difficult for a Democrat-Catholic to believe the first Catholic president in American history was harboring a pack of Communists at the highest levels of government.[9] Conversely, many fundamentalists who gave only limited support to McCarthy-led anticommunism because they disliked the senator's Catholicism were able to to participate during the 60's far more freely within far right circles since Catholic leadership no longer predominated there.

The movement of the early 1950's had nowhere near the high degree of organization so characteristics of the far right. By choice the senator was himself virtually the entire crusade. A decade later, hundreds of programs engaged the energies and funds of far rightists in all sections of the country. The leaders employed highly-skilled public relations experts to create an image of respectability and patriotism. They used publishing houses, TV and radio networks, bookstores, occasional political parties, and a cohesive, logical chain of command through all levels of operations.[10]

(Garden City, N. Y.: Doubleday & Co., Anchor Books, 1964), pp. 377, 379.

[9] Roy, "Conflict from the Communist Left and the Radical Right," in *Religion and Social Conflict,* eds. Martin E. Marty and Robert Lee (New York: Oxford University Press, 1964), p. 63; Lipset, "Three Decades of the Radical Right," pp. 404-6; Vincent P. De Santis, "American Catholics and McCarthyism," *Catholic Historical Review* LI (1965), 1-20.

[10] For information on the few organizations then in operation which became well-known radical right programs, see Wilbur H. Baldinger, "Reading from the Right," *The Progressive* (June, 1956), 5-8; Gordon D. Hall, "Patriotism on the Far Right," *Social Progress* XLVI (April, 1956), 5-26.

Finally, the passage of time helped to weaken enthusiasm for some causes and to create fresh energy for others. Primary among the latter was the demand for equal civil rights. Much of the leadership for Freedom, Now! came from the National Council of Churches and its member denominations. The far right bitterly resented that leadership and built much of its program around antiintegrationist sentiment. The civil rights movement, as will be discussed below, was crucial in the development of the radical right. Such sentiment was scarcely visible in the 1950's during the reign of Senator McCarthy.

Somewhere among the clusters of doctrines, theories, emotions, and suspicions that swirled across the nation in 1958, there emerged the hard core of far right ideology and practice. No national convention was held, no one house organ or journal spoke for every faction, no single individual appeared to take full command.

At the outset the leaders and supporters of the ACCC–ICCC did not assert bold leadership among the potential radical right. As similar as was their political and economic ideology to that of their nonseparated brothers, they could not ignore their commitment to uphold verbal inspiration, to walk the road of total separation, and to defend their premillennialism. Their suspicion of everyone outside their tradition taught them to be watchful, lest even those who appeared to be God-fearing, loyal patriots might turn out to be Satan's lieutenants.

These convictions prevented any early organic union of ultrafundamentalists with the general far right. However, as both groups soon came to realize, they were moving in the same direction along parallel tracks. So intensive would their fear of the internal conspiracy become, that by 1961 they would find themselves coupled together in a solemn crusade. To understand how the four major spokesmen of the church-related far right were able to bring their programs from obscurity into national prominence during the early 1960's, it is helpful to look briefly at the history of each organization.

From its beginnings in 1936, ultrafundamentalism had been shaped and inspired by Dr. Carl McIntire.[11] The Twentieth Cen-

[11] The authorized biography is in a pamphlet, Clarence Laman, "God Calls a Man"; he was awarded an honorary doctorate in divinity by Toronto Baptist

67

tury Reformation program has been built on the many resources he and his associates have at their command. From the base at Collingswood, New Jersey, McIntire has used the weekly *Christian Beacon* newspaper, a thirty-minute, five-times-weekly radio program (expanding from one to some six hundred stations between 1958 and 1964), Shelton and Highland colleges, the post-1956 separated Bible Presbtyerian Church Association, and the American and International Councils for promoting the message of ultra-fundamentalism.

All of these programs, except the broadcasting, existed before 1958, but only rarely had they attracted national attention. The collections for that year totalled some $62,000. In the next three years when the far right expanded across the nation, those receipts increased over tenfold, reaching some $635,000 by the end of 1961.[12]

The rapid increase can be traced to the increased number of national issues raised by the ultrafundamentalists. Their leaders found little widespread concern over their old ecclesiastical polemics against the National Association of Evangelicals or over their foreign missions controversies. They noted, instead, that when their radio broadcasts, public rallies, or publications spoke out on broad national problems their receipts increased accordingly.

Dr. McIntire carefully avoided any direct political involvement in his messages. However he did not avoid completely a degree of political involvement himself. In 1945 he had written: "the ministry of the church is to be missionary, not governmental. It is not the business of the church to run the world. Church and state must be separate." In 1961, with the onrushing tide of the far right being felt, he accepted an appointment to membership on the "National Advisory Board of Outstanding Americans" of the Young Americans for Freedom, a group devoted to advocating the passage of certain proposals and to electing specific individuals to office.[13]

Seminary in 1950, and an honorary Doctor of Letters in 1952 from Bob Jones College, now Bob Jones University.

[12] Group Research, Inc., "The Finances of the Far Right," pp. 5, 7.

[13] McIntire, *Twentieth Century Reformation*, rev. ed., p. 131; letter from David R. Jones of the national office of YAF to Erling Jorstad, July 22, 1965. In its own words, the YAF "worked for conservative candidates in over 1,000

McIntire's rise to prominence received sharp criticism from some prominent conservative leaders. In the late 1950's, at least two of the most influential spokesmen for the right wing expressed their distaste. J. Howard Pew of Sun Oil, and financier of many conservative programs, wrote to a fellow conservative, James D. Clise, in Oregon:

Unfortunately, Carl McIntire is a trouble maker. Everybody is always wrong but himself. It makes no difference how conservative a man may be, unless he goes all the way down the line with Carl McIntire, he is a scoundrel and a crook. As a result, he has sacrificed almost every minister of whatever faith or belief.[14]

The founder of Spiritual Mobilization and pastor of the First Congregational Church in Los Angeles, James W. Fifield, wrote about McIntire: "I do not consider him a responsible person, I do not go along with many of his points of view." [15]

McIntire showed little public concern with criticisms from conservatives or anyone else. In the last three years of the 1950's, he helped several colleagues start their own anti-Communist programs. The most successful early offshoot was the Christian Anti-Communism Crusade of Dr. Fred C. Schwarz, the Australian physician. In his first years in America, he worked closely with the ultrafundamentalists, speaking on McIntire's radio broadcast, lecturing at ACCC–ICCC congregations, and accepting an appointment to the ICCC Commission on International Relations.

As his crusade picked up momentum, Schwarz carefully moved away from any direct identification with the American or International Councils. He avoided any discussion of total separation; he made no direct appeal to fundamentalists although he affirmed his loyalty to their basic doctrines; he made no overt

_____
separate campaigns for local, state and national offices." See also Hofstadter, *The Paranoid Style*, pp. 72-77.

[14] Pew to James W. Clise, March 25, 1958, a letter deposited in the Clise Papers, University of Oregon, as quoted in Eckard V. Toy, "Ideology and Conflict in American Ultraconservatism, 1945-1960," (Ph.D. diss., University of Oregon, 1965), p. 94.

[15] Fifield to Clise, March 25, 1958, Clise Papers, University of Oregon, as quoted in Toy, "Ideology and Confict," p. 94.

connection between God's will and America as the Chosen Nation; and his premillennialism was expressed in highly muted tones. By 1964, he had moved more directly into the conservative camp, engaging Ivy League university professors for his conferences and associating with persons the ACCC–ICCC considered apostate; he had separated from the separationists.[16]

Dr. McIntire's many-sided program was largely responsible for inspiring two other ICCC colleagues into forming their own enterprises, Dr. Billy James Hargis and Christian Crusade and Mr. Edgar C. Bundy and the Church League of America. These operations, which took their present form in the late 1950's, reflect in almost every significant respect the theology, ideology, and action programs of the Twentieth Century Reformation. The formal binding element among the three groups was their mutual membership in the International Council of Christian Churches.[17]

Billy James Hargis was born in Texarkana, Texas, in 1925. By his own admission, he "never was willing to really study in school." After high school he matriculated in Ozark Bible College in 1943, the same year he was ordained into the ministry. At Ozark he remained for a year and a half but left before receiving grades in his courses. Later in life he stated his real education was obtained "in the university of hardknocks."[18]

[16] Summarized from my article, "The Remodeled Right: Schwarz and Stormer on Campus," *motive* XXVI (Nov., 1965), 29-32; *Christian Beacon,* April 24, 1958, pp. 1, 8; Janson and Eismann, *The Far Right,* pp. 50-55; McIntire, *Servants of Apostasy,* p. 377.

[17] Although all students of ultrafundamentalism acknowledge the obviously close relations between Bundy and McIntire, some see Hargis and McIntire more as competitors than allies. Whatever competition there is did not come into public view until after 1964. The group to which Hargis belongs which is in the ICCC is the International Conference of Calvary Tabernacles, also known as the Southwest Radio Church of the Air; it does not belong to the ACCC; see the *Christian Beacon,* Sept. 2, 1965, p. 7, and Nov. 5, 1964, p. 8; letter of Dr. Hargis to Erling Jorstad, July 15, 1965.

[18] Fernando Penebaz, *Crusading Preacher from the West* (Tulsa: Christian Crusade Press, 1965), p. 41; Hargis, *The Weekly Crusader,* March 9, 1962, p. 7. At Ozark he enrolled in Evidences, Advanced English, Old Testament History, Homiletics, Public Speaking, and Acts of the Apostles. On the back of his registration card an Ozark official wrote: "1/3 years Ozark Bible College." The president of the college stated this meant Hargis left school before he received grades for these courses; see Harold William Cook, "A Critical Analysis of the Use of Emotion as a Technique of Persuasion in Selected Anti-Communist Speeches of Dr. Billy James Hargis" (Master of Arts thesis, no. 927, Bowling Green State University, 1963), pp. 21-27.

After serving small rural parishes for a few years, he moved in 1947 to Sapulpa, Oklahoma, where he founded Christian Crusade. He was converted to an anti-Communist ministry in Sapulpa, stating he was "called of God to launch a mass movement of resistance to the trend in American life to world government, apostate religion, and appeasement with satanic 'isms' such as communism." [19]

Most of his energies in the early 50's centered on a four radio station network and in the Bible Balloon Project for the ICCC, his first face-to-face work with Dr. McIntire. He was also named to the Radio and Audio Film Commission of the International Council and carried on the balloon work for another five summers.[20]

A new public relations director, several honorary degrees (some from diploma mills), articles published in the *American Mercury*, and world traveling helped Hargis move Christian Crusade into greater prominence in the late 1950's. In 1958, his first major publication appeared: "The National Council of Churches Indicts Itself on Fifty Counts of Treason Against God and Country." Receipts rose quickly for the head crusader, corresponding closely to the growth of the far right across the nation.[21] Much of the success was due to increased efficiency in promotion. Hargis offered free tracts on his radio broadcasts. As the requests came in, the name of the listener was added to a solicitation fund. The public relations office charted the mailings to determine which offers and publications attracted the largest

[19] Penebaz, *Crusading Preaching*, p. 54; much on the events in Sapulpa is in Pete Martin, "I Call on Billy James Hargis," *Christian Herald*, Feb. 1967, pp. 74-76; there is an autobiographical sketch with photographs in *Christian Crusade*, Nov., 1965, pp. 27-28.

[20] Forster and Epstein, *Danger on the Right*, pp. 71-72; Penebaz, *Crusading Preacher*, pp. 55-56 and chap. 7; a Christian Crusade pamphlet by Richard Briley, "The Untold Story of the Bible Balloons"; *New York Times*, Aug. 6, 1961, p. 13; Welch, *The Politician*, p. 155; Hargis, "A Christian Ambassador," *American Mercury* LXXXV (Oct., 1957), 142-43; Hargis, *Communist America*, chaps. 5-6; Martin, "I Call on Hargis," *Christian Herald*, March, 1967, pp. 29, 30, 68-71; the autumn issues of the *Christian Beacon* for 1953 contain information on the balloon projects.

[21] As reported by Donald Quinn, writing in *The Oklahoma Courier* (a Roman Catholic diocese paper); the article by Quinn was entered in the U. S., Congress, Senate, *Congressional Record*, 87th Cong., 1st sess., 1962, 108, pt. 5, 6576-80; Penebaz, *Crusading Preacher*, pp. 59-62; Cook, "A Critical Analysis," pp. 22-24; Hargis, "Three Christian Giants in a World of Dwarfs," *American Mercury* LXXXV (Dec., 1957), 14, 17, 19.

number of requests. Television and radio time was purchased on the basis of the contributions produced through the mail.[22]

"The best break we ever got" for Hargis appeared unexpectedly in 1960 when the "Air Force Manual Scandal" attracted considerable press, radio, and television coverage. The memberships and contributions to the Tulsa office nearly doubled when it became known that a civilian, Homer H. Hyde, had drawn from Hargis and other sources to produce an Air Force manual tracing pro-Communist motivations to the National Council of Churches, contributors to the Revised Standard Version of the Bible, and other standard targets of ultrafundamentalist criticism. The NCC protested bitterly against what it considered to be unfounded charges and the Air Force withdrew the manual. Dr. McIntire and Mr. Bundy stoutly defended the charges and stated the Hargis materials were fully accurate.[23]

From that point on Christian Crusade increased its receipts substantially to where it ranked second only to the Twentieth Century Reformation. It contributed powerfully to the growth of the fundamentalism of the far right; its program was similar to that of Dr. McIntire in most respects. There were observable differences, however. Dr. Hargis encouraged members of the National Association of Evangelicals to participate in Christian Crusade; a past president, in fact, has been a feature crusade speaker. By contrast, no NAE speaker has ever been invited to address any program of the Twentieth Century Reformation. Dr. Hargis also worked outside the framework of existing denominations. His cathedral in Tulsa has been advertised as a nondenominational center for church-goers, but he discouraged members of NCC to worship there. Dr. McIntire, on the other hand, has worked almost exclusively within organized ecclesiastical circles. Dr. Hargis has also chosen to identify his movement and himself directly with other nonchurch-related far right groups. He was an early member of such groups as the John Birch Society as well as of We, the People!, Liberty Lobby, and the National Indigna-

[22] Group Research, Inc., "Finances of the Far Right," pp. 5, 7; Quinn in *Congressional Record*, 1962, pp. 6577-79; *Christian Crusade*, July, 1964, p. 2 has a story explaining the operations of the radio programs and finances.
[23] The quote is from Harold H. Martin, "Doomsday Merchants of the Far Right," *Saturday Evening Post*, April 29, 1962, p. 24; Penebaz, *Crusading Preacher*, pp. 258-61; see pp. 83-84.

tion Convention.[24] Dr. McIntire has largely limited his activities to the programs of the ACCC–ICCC.

These are the only major differences between the two crusades. They stand firmly united on their theology, ideology, and judgments on the major issues of the day. Dr. McIntire wrote to Hargis, "I think of you often and remember you in prayer and rejoice in the wonderful way in which God is using you." [25]

The other major program which came into prominence through the inspiration of Dr. McIntire is the Church League of America (CLA), Wheaton, Illinois, headed by Mr. (or "Major") Edgar C. Bundy. Although the league was founded in 1937, it did not achieve national prominence until after its identification with the ACCC–ICCC, when in 1956 Mr. Bundy became its executive secretary.

Edgar C. Bundy was born in Connecticut in 1915. He graduated from Wheaton College with a B.A. in 1938. He joined the Army in 1941 and earned a commission as a second lieutenant in October, 1942. He was ordained into the Baptist ministry in the Southern Baptist Convention in the spring of 1942. During six years of active military duty, he rose to the rank of major, serving in most theaters of operation and receiving several citations. His highest post was "Chief of Research and Analysis of the Intelligence Section, Headquarters, Alaskan Air Command in 1948 and a Briefing Officer for the Command." During that year he resigned to enter journalism in Wheaton, Illinois.[26]

Bundy soon identified himself with the American Council of

[24] *Christian Crusade,* March, 1966, p. 28; the NAE speaker was Dr. Frederick Curtis Fowler of Duluth, Minnesota; see a Christian Crusade booklet, "Highlights: Christian Crusade Third Annual Anti-Communist Leadership School, 1964," pp. 8-9; for more information on the interlocking of these groups see pp. 104-14.

[25] Penebaz, *Crusading Preacher,* p. 233. Hargis at one time supported Billy Graham but on his radio program of April 12, 1966, he sharply criticized the noted evangelist for not "separating from apostasy," and later for leading Christians into the ecumenical movement; *Christian Crusade,* March, 1967, p. 27. The most thorough study of Hargis' ideas is John H. Redekop, *The American Far Right: A Case Study of Billy James Hargis and Christian Crusade* (Grand Rapids: Eerdmans Publishing Co., 1968).

[26] The authorized "Biographical Data" is in an undated pamphlet, "What is the Church League of America?" pp. 6-7; this source does not disclose the nature of Mr. Bundy's theological training. A more recent publication containing more information is "Price List for Publications of the Church League of America" (n.d.), pp. 12-14, [hereafter cited as "Price List"].

73

Christian Churches. By 1949, he had published an article in the *Christian Beacon* containing the standard charges against the Federal Council of Churches, Harry Emerson Fosdick, the social gospel, and apostasy. Shortly thereafter he joined McIntire's group as a part-time public relations official and researcher.[27]

He also testified at that time before the United States Senate Appropriations Committee on the invitation of Senator Kenneth McKellar. He spoke on the "entire Far Eastern situation, including China, Siberia, Japan, Manchuria, Korea, the Philippines, Southeast Asia, and Alaska." He was able to do this in two hours of the hearing, which was read into the *Congressional Record* by Senators Styles Bridges, Pat McCarran, and Chairman McKellar. From that time on, Bundy found himself in demand for lectures to civic, patriotic, church, school, and fraternal groups.[28]

This entry into ultraconservative political and religious circles occurred during the rise to prominence of Senator Joseph R. McCarthy. Bundy found subversion within the State Department and the United Nations; he found members of the National Council of Churches preparing to overthrow American capitalism; he headed the ACCC–ICCC delegation at the hearing of the House Un-American Activities Committee on Bishop Oxnam, and was quoted by an NCC pamphlet as saying that the Wisconsin senator was "the greatest man alive" and "I like McCarthy and his methods." [29]

In 1956, the board of directors of the Church League of America appointed Bundy as the new executive director. They believed the league would have to do everything in its power to combat the internal conspiracy, now galloping ahead at a perilous rate. They agreed wholeheartedly with McIntire and Matthews

---

[27] *Christian Beacon,* May 19, 1949, *passim;* Edward Cain, *They'd Rather Be Right: Youth and the Conservative Movement* (New York: The Macmillan Co., 1963), p. 209; "Sowing Dissension in the Churches," an undated twenty-four page mimeographed report by the Department of Christian Social Relations, The Protestant Episcopal Church, p. 4; Roy, *Apostles of Discord,* pp. 240-41, 402-3.

[28] "Price List," p. 13.

[29] National Council of Churches, "The Truth About the Churches," a pamphlet, as reprinted in McIntire's rebuttal pamphlet, "The Truth About the Churches . . ." (n.d.), p. 18; Gasper, *The Fundamentalist Movement,* pp. 59, 69; Roy, *Apostles of Discord,* pp. 240-42; Cain, *They'd Rather Be Right,* pp. 209-10; "Sowing Dissension," pp. 4-6.

that the most sinister threat to America lay with the churches.[30]

To combat this the league would collect, analyze, and disseminate information, prepared especially for clergymen, on those political, religious, economic, and social activities which the leaguers considered contrary to their understanding of the Christian foundations of free enterprise and self-government. In its own words, its chief resources were the "thousands of files of individuals and organizations who have been engaged in subversive or 'fellow-traveler' activities." The directors also chose to keep files on organizations not on the attorney general's list, such as the Americans for Democratic Action, the American Civil Liberties Union, and the Fellowship of Reconciliation.

Once at the controls, Bundy quickly expanded the league's programs in several directions. He took great care to prevent the identification of the CLA with any organization other than the ACCC–ICCC. To this day Bundy states the Church League has "absolutely no connection with the John Birch Society," or other comparable groups.[31]

The most unique feature of the enterprise has been the research files. These contain material on Communists, fellow travelers, sympathizers, dupes, and joiners of fronts. The most extensive single collection are the files of Dr. J. B. Matthews. Some critics have pointed out that such investigative work is the responsibility of only the F.B.I. Bundy answers by stating the league is not to blame for the records made by the suspects and the league only furnishes evidence collected by the federal government as well as by his organization. Readers of CLA reports thus have additional information at their disposal to combat the internal conspiracy.[32]

In another direction, Bundy has turned the monthly News and Views into a major source of information for ultrafundamentalists and far rightists. Many issues have become their standard interpretations of major issues. The league's "Price List" offers items on a wide variety of subjects: Union Theological Seminary, the Reuther brothers, subversive mental health programs, ultrafunda-

[30] "Price List," p. 3.
[31] News and Views, March, 1965, p. 7; see pp. 111-12 for the "connections" with the John Birch Society.
[32] "Price List," passim; News and Views, Feb. 1965, p. 13.

mentalist criticism of the NCC and WCC, extensive attacks on creeping liberalism in the Episcopalian, Baptist, Presbyterian, and Lutheran churches, denunciation of critics of the far right (such as Gordon Hall, Arthur Larson, Ralph Lord Roy, and G. Bromley Oxnam), and rejection of pacifism, Protestants and Other Americans United for Separation of Church and State, Billy Graham, and John Foster Dulles. Filmstrips for sale include "Operation Abolition," "Communism on the Map," "Ronald Reagan on the Welfare State," and "The Truth About Communism" narrated by Ronald Reagan.

Mr. Bundy has produced several full-length books dealing with the same general problems. His first, *Collectivism in the Churches,* 1958, shows his acceptance of total separation. He called on "the true Christian" to follow 2 Cor. 6:17, "come out from among them and be separate, saith the Lord, and touch not the unclean thing." He believes the American businessmen who believe in the American way of life should separate from the ecumenical churches and support the small, independent congregations and ministers. The greatest example of separationism was Jesus, a "fundamentalist" himself who ignored the religious authorities and "social action" committees of his day.[33]

The Church League of America has established itself as a significant influence in helping shape the opinions of fundamentalists of the far right. It generally avoids overlapping and duplicating the programs of Drs. McIntire and Hargis, and has been a powerful voice in advancing the ideology and programs of ultrafundamentalism.

The last and, financially speaking, the smallest of the nationally influential ultrafundamentalist groups to make itself known in the late 1950's was the American Council of Christian Laymen (ACCL). Founded by Verne P. Kaub in Madison, Wisconsin, in 1950, it changed its name and affiliation to the "Laymen's Commission of the American Council of Christian Churches" after Kaub's death in 1964. It is a constituent organization within the

---

[33] Bundy, *Collectivism in the Churches,* pp. viii, 229. For some strong criticism of Bundy's theology by a conservative spokesman see the letters of Edmund Opitz, of the Foundation for Economic Education, to James C. Clise, quoted in Toy, "Ideology and Conflict," p. 96.

ACCC, and thus holds formal membership within the ultrafunda-mentalist movement.

Several qualifications about Mr. Kaub should be made at the outset. He alone of the four major leaders was not ordained. He was a member, apparently an unhappy member, of the First Congregational Church in Madison.[34] He was the only one of the four ACCC–ICCC leaders who was anti-Semitic.

Kaub was born in 1884 in Michigan and received his public school education there and in Indiana. In 1905, he began two years of study at the University of Wisconsin. He later took up surveying, sales work, factory labor, and newspaper reporting. He started editorial work and continued until 1935. He joined the public relations staff of the Wisconsin Power and Light Company. After retiring in 1949, he founded the American Council of Christian Laymen.[35]

Before making anticommunism his chief interest, Kaub mixed heavily in several anti-Semitic organizations during the 1940's. He was deeply involved in what Arnold Forster of the Anti-Defamation League has called the "outrageously un-American Chicago organization, Citizens U.S.A. Committee." "In 1943," Forster writes, "Kaub was Western representative for Joe Kamp's Constitutional Educational League. He was a frequent contributor to the bitterly anti-Jewish hate sheet, *The Individualist*." [36] When the zealous anti-Semitic editor of *Common Sense*, Conde McGinley, died, Kaub wrote in an undated ACCL news letter that McGinley had been a dedicated servant of the Master and whose "passing is a great loss to the cause of human liberty." *Common Sense* returned the compliment when Kaub died.[37]

In 1946, Kaub entered the ranks of ultraconservatism with his first book, *Collectivism Challenges Christianity*. A favorable in-

[34] Erwin A. Gaede, "The Federal Council of Churches of Christ in America: The Evolution of Social Policy" (Master of Arts thesis, University of Wisconsin, 1951), pp. 90-94.

[35] See the inside front cover page of his two books: *Communist-Socialist Propaganda in American Schools* (Madison: American Council of Christian Laymen, 1960), and *Collectivism Challenges Christianity* (Madison: American Council of Christian Laymen, 1961); Gaede, "The FCC," pp. 90-94.

[36] Arnold Forster, *A Measure of Freedom* (Garden City, N. Y.: Doubleday & Co., 1950), pp. 74-79.

[37] A letter from the Madison office entitled "We Take No Vacations"; *Common Sense*, Nov. 1, 1964, p. 3.

77

troduction for it was made by the Rev. Harold John Ockenga, a major voice within the National Association of Evangelicals. The review blurbs on the back cover of the 1961 edition indicate that several reputable denominational publishing firms used the advertising copy for it from the publisher.

This prominent beginning took on significance in light of Kaub's next major contribution. After retirement from public relations in 1949, he and some associates began research on what would become his most explosive contribution, "How Red is the Federal (National) Council of Churches?" the all-time ultrafundamentalist best seller. The reading public was not given the full information, however, about the authorship of the pamphlet when it appeared in 1950. Among his associates Kaub had given the principal responsibility for research to Allan Anderson Zoll, another well-known anti-Semitic writer and fellow officer of an organization called the National Council for American Education, plus J. B. Matthews, the well-traveled researcher. These two contributed to "How Red . . . ?" [38] Neither Zoll nor Matthews nor any one else was listed as the author. Perhaps one reason for the absence of Zoll's name was that he already was on the United States Attorney General's list of subversive organizations for membership in a group known as the American Patriots, Inc.[39]

The book and the pamphlet placed Kaub solidly in the center of McCarthy-inspired anticommunism in the early 1950's. Zoll appointed Kaub as vice-president in charge of research of the National Council for American Education. The ACCL in 1953 published the result, Kaub's *Communist-Socialist Propoganda in*

[38] Matthews himself showed no anti-Semitic tendencies: Forster, *A Measure of Freedom*, pp. 77-78; Gaede, "The FCC," pp. 90-94; see the discussions of Zoll in Arnold Forster and B. R. Epstein, *The Troublemakers* (Garden City, N. Y.: Doubleday & Co., 1952), pp. 199-200, 207-8, 212-13, 104; Mary Anne Raywid, *The Ax-Grinders: Critics of Our Public Schools* (New York: The Macmillan Co., 1963), pp. 164-70.

[39] Forster and Epstein, *Danger on the Right*, p. 79. A link to Hargis develops here. In the early 1960's he purchased the files previously owned by Zoll and American Patriots. Hargis apparently already knew these materials contained the "names of thousands of clergymen and educators who had chosen to affiliate with communist front organizations over the years"; Harry and Bonaro Overstreet, *The Strange Tactics*, pp. 198-99. Unfortunately, the Penebaz biography has no information on this purchase.

American Schools.[40] This clearly was Kaub's most cherished subject. He attacked the National Educational Association, progressive education, John Dewey, and everyone else promoting "the ideology of Communism-socialism."

Kaub's solution for many of the problems created by communism-socialism was offered in an NCAE pamphlet, "How Red Are the Schools?" He advocated a full restoration of McGuffey Readers on every age level for which the readers were available. His council in Madison offered the latest revisions of the 1879 edition at $20 for a six volume set.

In his later years he gave full attention to offering a complete line of books, pamphlets, and information about common interests to far rightists; he sold titles by Hargis, the Circuit Riders, Kenneth Goff, Bundy, McIntire, and Robert Welch, as well as criticisms of the RSV Bible, the civil rights movement, and World Council of Churches.

The Madison author also made long range plans for the ACCL. He learned in 1963 that the ACCC had established a "Laymen's Conference" designed to reach the man in the pew with the major issues of the day. After discussing their mutual interests and realizing how close their programs were, leaders of the Laymen's Council and Kaub agreed to merge. Now near eighty, Kaub dissolved the ACCL and turned it over as a gift to the ACCC. He was to have a leading role in the new program. Just then, in September, 1964, he died. The new leaders established headquarters in Pittsburgh to carry on the Kaubian tradition of "opposition to the inroads made by Communism into America, liberalism and apostasy in the churches, and . . . the socializing influence exerted by the forces of evil." Their first labor was a reissue of ten thousand copies of "How Red . . . ?" Their office also distributed the complete line of ACCL pamphlets as well as all ACCC materials.[41] The merger was complete.

In summation, the cleavage within fundamentalism following the 1942 split at St. Louis led the ACCC to practice total separa-

[40] For a critical judgment of Kaub's views see Raywid, *The Ax-Grinders,* pp. 12, 47, 68, 169-70.

[41] An ACCL promotional flyer entitled "6 for 5, Bonus Book Offer" (n.d.), p. 2; a mimeographed letter by George F. Kurtz, Chairman to "Friends of the ACCC" dated September, 1964, Pittsburgh, Pa., and an undated mimeographed letter by Kurtz to this group written during the later fall of 1964.

tion. When its leaders incorporated far right ideology into their ultrafundamentalist theology, they came to see themselves as the only pure anti-Communist, church-related witness within American Protestantism. To them, both the NAE and the NCC were soft on communism. The forces of the cold war and the enthusiasm for the kind of investigations headed by Senator McCarthy helped unify the several far right elements in the early 1950's. His death and the continued concern for the state of American life contributed directly to the emergence of many far right organizations in the late 1950's. By then the experience gained by the ACCC-ICCC in support of Senator McCarthy's and related programs brought the fundamentalists of the far right into a position of leadership among church-related far rightists. The four most influential of these bodies, those discussed above, came to represent the union of the religious and political streams of the radical right. While suspicious of all nonseparationist bodies, the ultrafundamentalists attracted wide support. Within the next five years they would find reason to cooperate with other general far right groups. With the presidential campaign of 1964 the ultrafundamentalists would find themselves in the full stream of the radical right.

4

The Achievement of Power, 1961-64

When planning a tour of the West Coast for November, 1961, President John F. Kennedy chose Los Angeles as the site for a major address. Among the issues to be raised would be a response to his critics on the far right, whose numbers were heavily concentrated in the City of the Angels. Early in the speech he issued the challenge.

In the most critical periods of our Nation's history, there have always been those on the fringes of our society who have sought to escape their own responsibility by finding a simple solution, an appealing slogan or a convenient scapegoat.

And under the strains and frustrations imposed by constant tension and harassment, the discordant voices of extremism are heard once again in the land. Men who are unwilling to face up to the dangers from without are convinced that the real danger comes from within.

They look suspiciously at their neighbors and their leader. They call for a "man on horseback" because they do not trust the people. They find treason in our churches, in our highest court, in our treatment of water. They equate the Democratic Party with the welfare state, the welfare state with socialism, socialism with communism. They object quite rightly to politics intruding on the military—but they are anxious for the military to engage in politics. Let our patriotism be reflected in the creation of confidence in one another, rather than in crusades of suspicion. . . . Above all, let us remember, however serious the outlook, however harsh the task, the one great irreversible trend in the history of the world is on the side of liberty.[1]

From Tulsa a few months later the challenge was hurled back by Dr. Hargis:

Those influences in Washington today are pro-communist, parading under the name of liberal. This nation today is in the hands of a group of Harvard radicals who have long ago been "hooked" by the insidious dope of socialism and view human life from the international standpoint. Their hearts bleed for the whole world—EXCEPT FOR THE UNITED STATES OF AMERICA. They are a dangerous scourge—and they are so deeply entrenched in power that they can be removed only by a nationwide upsurge of conservatism—which, please God, will come in the elections of next November.

It makes no differences whatever that these Harvard eggheads call themselves Democrats or Republicans. This has now become a distinction without a difference. They are liberals; liberals are socialists; and Khrushchev himself said that socialism is "the first phase of communism." [2]

The far right and ultrafundamentalist movements might never have developed into multimillion dollar enterprises, nor

---

[1] *New York Times,* Nov. 19, 1961, p. 54; Arthur M. Schlesinger, Jr., *A Thousand Days: John F. Kennedy in the White House* (Boston: Houghton Mifflin, 1965), p. 753; Theodore C. Sorensen, *Kennedy* (New York: Harper & Row, 1965), p. 355.

[2] *The Weekly Crusader,* June 1, 1962, p. 2.

indeed surpassed their five-figure incomes, had not John F. Kennedy, and all that he represented, become president at that moment in history. The radical right found in his principles, his personality, and the accomplishments of his administration the ideal embodiment of the internal conspiracy. He was the perfect target: Roman Catholic, Harvard, intellectual, Boston-accented, sophisticated, very wealthy, liberal, and consistently good copy for the mass media. Mrs. Kennedy heightened his public presence with her elegance and poise; the brothers and sisters all reinforced the image. Spokesmen for the fundamentalist of the far right would recognize how the Kennedy style would infuriate their supporters. They would also learn how to attract new revenue by presenting themselves as America's only real antidote to the venomous New Frontier.

The best proof of this is found in the financial growth of the three leading ultrafundamentalist groups along with three prominent far right enterprises.[3] (The figures represent thousands of dollars).

	1961	1962	1963	1964
Twentieth Century Reformation	635.5	1,163.0	1,718.0	3,000.+
Christian Crusade	817.2	775.4	677.2	834.8
Church League of America	196.0	200.4	235.6	208.6
Human Events	918.5	1,005.9	927.5	not known
Americans for Constitutional Action	61.2	145.7	84.9	187.4
John Birch Society	595.9	826.1	1,092.3	3,200.0

The first clear signs of ACCC–ICCC opposition to Mr. Kennedy as a presidential candidate appeared early in 1960 during the uproar over the Air Force Training Manual. At first the argument seemed to be only one more clash between the ultrafundamentalists and the National Council of Churches over the familiar topics of "Red clergy," the Revised Standard Version, and social involvement of the churches. The newspapers showed little interest.

Then, suddenly, the manual turned into a major issue when

[3] Group Research, "The Finances of the Far Right," pp. 5, 8; *New York Times*, June 28, 1965, p. 22; *Time*, Feb. 12, 1965, p. 65; *Time*, Aug. 27, 1965, pp. 59-60; *National Observer*, Oct. 31, 1966, p. 5.

Senator Kennedy, already an announced presidential candidate, gave his full support to the NCC and the Secretary of the Air Force. Now the press took notice. Here was a controversy between a Roman Catholic, whose every word on religion was closely studied by the public, and a group of Protestant clergymen, who had already labeled Catholicism as the "Harlot of Babylon" and as more tyrannical than communism. The ultrafundamentalists found themselves back on the front pages of the newspapers for the first time since the early 1950's, and they attempted to capitalize on the opportunity. The leaders issued frequent, harshly worded press releases condemning vote-seeking politicians and weak-kneed apostates who claimed to be Christians. The only real believers were those who knew every answer was in the inerrant Bible and who had the courage to separate totally from sin.[4]

These and similar charges made good copy. The mass media found the public deeply interested in any Kennedy-Protestant squabble, and for several days gave the ACCC statements considerable publicity. Then, quietly the senator and the NCC moved on to different issues and the matter faded out of sight.

The leaders of the American Council tried to revive public attention. During the height of the presidential primaries they passed a resolution:

The Roman Church has already dedicated the United States to the Virgin Mary, and a Roman Catholic leader in the White House will advance that goal. Also, we do not want to see the spectacle of a President kissing a Cardinal's ring as an act of obeisance to Roman Catholic temporal authority.[5]

[4] The best general survey is Berton Dulce and Edward J. Richter, *Religion and the Presidency: A Recurring American Problem* (New York: The Macmillan Co., 1962), chaps. 9-13; see McIntire's pamphlet, "The Truth," *passim,* and most of the issues of the *Christian Beacon* for the first half of 1960; Penebaz, *Crusading Preacher,* chap. 10; Claire Cox, *The New Time Religion* (Englewood Cliffs, N. J., Prentice-Hall, 1961), chap. 7; Roy, *Communism and the Churches,* pp. 418-20.

[5] *Christian Beacon,* May 5, 1960, p. 1; Oct. 27, 1960, *passim;* see the editorials on this subject during the campaign in this journal. For McIntire's reply to the charge of the Democratic party that he was a "major anti-Catholic extremist" in 1960, see Forster and Epstein, *Danger on the Right,* p. 109. An excellent analysis of the anti-Catholic theme in this campaign is by Bruce Felknor,

This statement was ignored by all the communications media.

Throughout the summer and autumn, voters in and out of the ACCC–ICCC raised searching questions about the senator's loyalties to Rome and America. Some pastors were honestly worried; others found their congregations responded with increased contributions to anti-Catholic sermons. Some far right groups, completely outside ultrafundamentalist circles, distributed scurrilous anti-Catholic materials. The Ku Klux Klan and American Nazi Party added their tinkling cymbals of dissent.[6]

From its inception to its tragic conclusion, the New Frontier offered the fundamentalists of the far right the evidence they sought to prove the strength of the internal conspiracy. Even before Inauguration Day, they fired their first barrage, aiming at the appointments of Chester Bowles, Adlai Stevenson, Dean Acheson, John Kenneth Galbraith, Arthur M. Schlesinger, Jr., and George Kennan. Here was prima facie proof the "Harvard radicals" hooked on liberalism-socialism-communism had already taken over the government.[7]

A few months later the disaster at the Bay of Pigs was seized on by the far right as the supreme example of Red domination at the highest levels of government. How else, its spokesmen asked, could one explain the defeat of the task force, the absence of air cover, and the appearance of Soviet weapons across Cuba? Why had not certain questions been answered: "How could Communists take over this island just 90 miles away?" or "Why don't we send in the Marines?" When the administration in 1962 moved to the brink of war to force the withdrawal of the Soviet arsenal from Cuba, the ultrafundamentalists retorted that this was only a token gesture to appease those Americans who feared stronger action.[8]

Dirty Politics (New York: W. W. Norton, 1966), pp. 55-65; he concludes that on this issue Mr. Nixon's policy "merits hearty applause."

[6] Dulce and Richter, *Religion and the Presidency,* chaps. 10-13; Franklin H. Littell, *From State Church to Pluralism: A Protestant Interpretation of Religion in American Life* (New York: Doubleday & Co., Anchor Books, 1962), pp. 151-55. H. L. Hunt, among other large financiers of the far right, invested heavily in anti-Catholic materials in 1960; *New York Times,* Aug. 17, 1964, p. 16.

[7] Sorensen, *Kennedy,* pp. 255-56.

[8] W. Cleon Skousen, *The Naked Communist,* 9th rev. ed. (Salt Lake City: Ensign Publishing Co., 1961), chap. 11; for background information on why they concluded that the United States helped Castro see the Christian Crusade

As further evidence of treason, the ACCC–ICCC spokesmen cited the decisions of the Supreme Court which, in their judgment, followed Moscow's line. They pointed to the sale of wheat to Russia, which was positive proof of their earlier suspicion that the New Frontier farm program, as well as the one of the Republicans, was strengthening communism around the globe. Only an internal conspiracy could explain the failure of Washington to prohibit its allies from trading with Communist nations, or for permitting Yugoslavia to train its pilots in America, or for the failure to tear down the Berlin wall. America's support of the United Nations, "that house of Red Babel," crippled its sovereignty and drained off taxpayers' dollars that should have been spent on more armaments.[9]

McIntire made his solution very clear. "Here is a speech of our President before the United Nations," he wrote, "saying that we must move into a realm of peaceful coexistence with the Communist world. . . . We have to fight it. We have to fight it from the White House on down. Wouldn't it be good if there was just some way to defeat Mr. Kennedy's reelection next time? " [10]

The mood of the radical right was becoming so bitter as to be susceptible to believing wild flights of fancy, as seen in the "Operation Water Moccasin" incident of 1962-63. A member of the John Birch Society speaker's bureau learned of a routine Army counterguerrilla training program being conducted in Georgia. Some of the trainees were members of the armies of

---

pamphlet, "Shall We Surrender to Castro or Smash Him?"; the most forthright statement on the internal conspiracy came from Rep. James B. Utt of California who wrote in a Christian Crusade pamphlet entitled "Who Are the Real Fright Peddlers?": "It is only human that some mistakes should be made but when none of them is in favor of America, I cannot help but recognize a design for surrender."

[9] See pp. 152-53 for a discussion of the Supreme Court; see the Hargis pamphlet "The Communist Program for the American Farmer"; *The Weekly Crusader*, July 20, 1962, pp. 5-8; *Christian Beacon*, June 24, 1965, p. 7. Most ultrafundamentalist publications of this period deal with one or more of these issues; see the Twentieth Century Reformation packet, "Tito's Blackmail Slave Labor"; *Christian Beacon*, Aug. 6, 1964, *passim*; the Christian Crusade pamphlets, "What's Wrong with America," "Lest We Forget," and "This I Believe"; *News and Views*, July, 1962; Kaub's general criticism is found in a reprint he distributed of an article of his in the Amarillo, Texas, *Daily News*, June 24, 1963.

[10] As quoted in John A. Stroman, "The American Council of Christian Churches" (Ph.D. diss., Boston University, 1966), p. 205.

American allies. To this observer the program became a sinister Communist plot to bring Reds, foreigners, one-worlders, and "barefooted Africans" here to destroy America. Senator Thomas Kuchel of California found through his mail and other sources that thousands of citizens wholeheartedly believed in the conspiratorial interpretation without questioning its source. In a few weeks the tumult subsided, but the episode suggested how deeply fearful many Americans had become of their own government.[11]

On top of this, the Army forced Major General Edwin A. Walker to resign because of his controversial citizenship education program for his troops. This was the final, ruthless stab in the hearts of Christian Americans. Who in their right mind could object to the inculcation of patriotic ideals into the hearts of the nation's fighting men? What loyal American could want to "muzzle the military" when it spoke for freedom? Why should the public object because some of the materials had been furnished by the John Birch Society or because one of the lecturers invited by Walker was Edgar C. Bundy of the Church League of America? Were these the acts of traitors? Dr. Hargis thought not. He enlisted Walker for a major speaking tour, "Operation Midnight Ride." Across the nation they called for an invasion of Cuba as well as repeating the familiar attacks on the New Frontier and the National Council of Churches.[12]

At rallies such as these, the spokesmen for the ultrafundamentalists found concrete evidence to support their beliefs that they were attracting contributors who were not necessarily members of an ACCC or ICCC group. For instance, McIntire discovered that as he added the New Frontier to his list of targets he was able to increase the number of radio stations carrying his program from

[11] See Kuchel's materials printed in the U. S., Congress, Senate; *Congressional Record*, 88th Cong., 1st sess., 1963, 109, pt. 6, 7632-42.

[12] Stroman, "The American Council of Christian Churches," pp. 205, 250-56; a Christian Crusade pamphlet, "The Muzzling of General Walker"; Walker's aide wrote a defense: Major Arch Roberts, *Victory Denied* (Chicago: Charles Hallberg and Co., 1966); Janson and Eismann, *The Far Right*, chap. 13; *The Christian Century*, March 27, 1963, p. 392; a full discussion of the relationships between the military and the far right is in John M. Swomley, Jr., *The Military Establishment* (Boston: Beacon Press, 1964), chap. 13; Pete Martin, "I Call on Billy James Hargis," *Christian Herald*, March, 1967, p. 72.

1 in 1958 to 540 by early 1964. His weekly journal also increased its circulation.[13]

In a similar manner Christian Crusade rejoiced over the increasing national publicity given its program. It concluded that the recent appearance of featured articles on Dr. Hargis in the *Post, Time, Newsweek,* and *Life* indicated strong support for the head crusader. It did not add that those articles were very critical.[14]

This expansion was characteristic of the entire radical right movement. Believing the administration was cowardly in its foreign policy and sensing the imminent destruction of all moral standards at home, thousands of citizens started to support the dozens of far right programs appearing everywhere. One study estimates that of the 282 groups operating by December, 1962, some 121 had been organized the previous year. Of these only 20 had been functioning before 1958.[15]

The increased revenue made possible further expansion through more radio programming, enlargement of office personnel, wider distribution of printed materials, and more public rallies. By late 1962 one could find a broad variety of programs. Some aimed at the whole of American life (We, the People!); others concentrated on a specific issue (the income tax, fluoridation); some concentrated on a specific organization (Methodist Laymen of North Hollywood). Some were quasi-legal at best, taking up arms for any contingency; others showed impeccable restraint by limiting their activities to erudite studies of economic theory.

Everywhere the market for films, lecturers, seminars, home study kits, and monthly discussion programs was insatiable. Funds

[13] *Christian Beacon,* Feb. 6, 1965, p. 1; a study by Group Research, Inc., "Periodicals on the Right," of Sept. 20, 1966, p. 20, shows the following circulation figures:

	1960	1961	1962	1963	1964
Christian Beacon	20,000	24,000	32,000	45,120	66,494
Christian Crusade	57,999	82,400	80,400	72,291	98,609
	(est.)	(est.)	(est.)		

Figures for the Church League of America and Kaub's Laymen were not available. Christian Crusade radio programs showed a similar pattern of growth; *Christian Crusade,* March, 1967, pp. 24-25.

[14] See the Christian Crusade tract, "You Can Fight Communism in Your Town."

[15] Richard Dudman, *Men of the Far Right* (New York: Pyramid Books, 1962), p. 16.

came from corporations and from individuals. The supporters apparently understood a full fledged new crusade, one which went far beyond the early McCarthy movement, was now rolling across the nation. It was broad enough to embrace many interests, yet unifed enough in its opposition to the New Frontier to provide a sense of cohesion and urgency.[16]

As the radical right expanded, President Kennedy and his associates stepped up their criticisms of the critics. In February, 1962, J. Edgar Hoover wrote:

> Far too many self-styled experts on communism are plying the highways of America, giving erroneous and distorted information. This causes hysteria, false alarms, misplaced apprehensions by many of our citizens. We need enlightenment about communism—but this information must be factual, accurate, and not tailored to echo personal idiosyncrasies.[17]

These statements only increased the intensity of the far-right criticism of the administration. Convinced that they were not "fright peddlers" nor "hate clubs," the ultrafundamentalists drew on new revenue in 1963 to expand their programs and facilities. However, the events of that year would bring about a profound alteration in both their outlook and their operations. Two developments especially helped produce a change of direction; the assassination of the president and the accelerated demands of Negroes for civil rights.

The mood of the nation, already deeply troubled over the Freedom Now! movment, was turned to horror when the news came from Dallas on November 22. This simply could not happen

[16] Alan F. Westin, "Anti-Communism and the Corporations," *Commentary* XXXVI (Dec., 1963), 479-87; Fletcher Knebel, "Rightist Revival: Who's Who on the Far Right," *Look*, March 13, 1962, pp. 21-31; *First National Directory of Rightist Groups, Publications, and Some Individuals in the U. S.*, 4th ed. (Sausalito, California: The Noontide Press, 1962). A useful bibliography is in "Current Bibliography and Abridged Directory of the American Right Wing," a fourteen-page mimeographed pamphlet published by the Kansas Free Press, Lawrence, Kansas (2nd ed., 1965).

[17] He did not mention any specific groups: "Shall It Be Law or Tyranny?" *American Bar Association Journal* XLVIII (Feb., 1962), p. 120. This statement by Hoover is not included in the many speeches of his distributed by the far right; see pp. 169-70.

in the mid-twentieth century; reasonable people did not behave that way.

At first the newsmen decided a far rightist had been the assassin. They found a paid statement in a Dallas morning newspaper accusing the president of treason and complicity with communism. Further, Dallas was a well-known haven for radical right activity. It seemed plausible that the political atmosphere there could spawn enough hate to trigger such a murder.

That error contributed strongly to the growth of the far right. It convinced its supporters (and perhaps some former fence straddlers) that the "Establishment" (official Washington) was in fact already attempting to destroy their programs, just as their arch enemy, Walter Reuther, had requested in 1961.[18] When the ties of Lee Harvey Oswald to the Soviet Union became known, the radical right leaders lashed back. They demanded apologies from their critics; they found the internal conspiracy at work in every phase of the plot to discredit them. Dr. McIntire offered a packet over the radio entitled "A Communist Kills Our President But the Right Wing is Blamed." [19]

The next few weeks gave the far right an unparalleled opportunity to recruit new support. The leaders, including those of the ACCC–ICCC, presented a twofold argument: Oswald was a Communist assassin acting on higher orders and, second, the internal conspiracy controlled the work of the Warren Commission.

The spokesmen found the first charge the more easy to document. The government soon published information about Oswald's life. To the far right, these added up to Communist espionage. The leaders concluded Jack Ruby was also a paid Red hatchetman, hired to silence the impulsive Oswald before he blurted out the whole story of Moscow's master plan. The John Birch Society announced that President Kennedy had "collaborated" with Chairman Khrushchev to stage a phony invasion of Cuba. Professor Revilo P. Oliver and Robert Welch argued that

[18] Perhaps the most complete statement by a far rightist on this point is by Billy James Hargis, The Far Left (Tulsa: Christian Crusade Press, 1964), chap. 5.
[19] Christian Beacon, Dec. 26, 1963, p. 1; Jan. 2, 1964, p. 4; Walker, The Christian Fright Peddlers, p. 264.

since the president was not converting America quickly enough to communism, Moscow had ordered his execution.[20] That conclusion, however, did not appear in the publications of the ultra-fundamentalists.

The attempt to link the Warren Commission with the internal conspiracy turned out to be more difficult. Evidence, however, was quickly produced. Dr. McIntire noted that President Lyndon Johnson had done what the *Daily Worker* had suggested— appoint Chief Justice Warren as head of a blue-ribbon commission to investigate and report on every phase of the assassination. The far right quickly took this cue for a renewed attack. To them Justice Warren was the incarnation of the most sinister, uncontrollable pro-Red forces at work in American life. Had not the "Warren Court" ordered integration, ended prayers in schools, restricted congressional investigations on subversion, and approved smutty literature? What else could the public expect from the Warren Commission than a complete whitewash of the real culprits for whom Oswald and Ruby were mere fronts? The presence on the commission of conservatives Senator Richard Russell and Representative Gerald Ford failed to quiet their anger. Even before the report appeared, Christian Crusade announced its conclusions in a pamphlet: "The Warren Report—I Won't Be Able to Trust It." [21]

To bring their facts to the public, McIntire, Hargis, and far right groups offered for sale a phonograph album of a radio debate held in New Orleans between Oswald and a Cuban refugee, Mr. Carlos Brunguier, concerning the Fair Play for Cuba Organization. They found links between Oswald and their perennial opponents, *The Christian Century* and the National Council of Churches. Dr. Hargis engaged Brunguier and Edwin A. Walker to lecture Crusader audiences on the meaning of the assassination. Walker told a group in Shreveport, Louisiana, that the death of President Franklin D. Roosevelt, the enrollment of James Meredith at the University of Mississippi, events in Viet Nam, and the slaying of President Kennedy were "all part of the same piece

[20] *New York Times,* March 15, 1964, p. 57.

[21] *Christian Beacon,* Dec. 26, 1963, p. 1; Jan. 2, 1964, p. 4; Jan. 28, 1965, p. 4; *Christian Crusade,* Aug. 1964, p. 24; a Christian Crusade pamphlet, "Oswald, A Castro Agent in the United States."

of cloth." He stated that an assassin also shot President Roosevelt as a part of the Communist world plot. Other Hargis publications hinted that "men in high places in Washington" would be exposed if the real facts of the slaying were published. Some of these facts were in the Brunguier pamphlet; some others were on a tape available from the Tulsa office for ten dollars. Among Oswald's several connections, Dr. Hargis found ties to Murder, Inc., the Mafia, and a tie-in between the American Nazi and American Communist parties.[22]

These charges were not altered by the publication of the Warren Commission Report. Its signers stated Oswald had acted independently without orders from any agency. This was adequate proof, in ultrafundamentalist judgment, that the predicted white-wash had materialized. In turn, the deep public interest in the assassination, the admission by Warren that not every last detail had been uncovered, and the whole aura of mystery so saturated in the deep emotional temper of the nation, all helped convince certain portions of the public, who were not necessarily members of the far right before November 22, that the internal conspiracy was responsible for it all.[23] The contributions to the far right grew larger.

The other major event of 1963 to alter the course of the radical right was the increased militancy of Negro demands for civil rights. Here the chronological order of the narrative must be interrupted and returned to the spring of 1963 when the Kennedy administration introduced the Civil Rights Bill into the Congress. To many citizens, the measure represented a belated recognition of the need to protect the opportunities of minority groups for unsegregated participation in American society. To the radical right and most ultrafundamentalists, however, the bill and its possible consequences stood as a sinister threat to the foundations

[22] *Christian Beacon,* Aug. 13, 1964, pp. 2, 6; Dec. 26, 1963, p. 1; Jan. 2, 1964, p. 4; see the newspaper account of Walker's speech reprinted in the Christian Crusade pamphlet; "Highlights: Christian Crusade Third Annual Anti-Communist Leadership School, 1964," p. 15; Hargis, Newsletter of March 15, 1964, datelined from Los Angeles. The ties to the Mafia, *et al.,* are reported in Forster and Epstein, *Danger on the Right,* p. 70; see also Hargis, *The Far Left,* chaps. 5, 9, and his February, 1964, Newsletter from Tulsa.

[23] A helpful summary in Dennis Brogan, "Death in Dallas," *Encounter* XXIII (Dec., 1964), 20-26.

of American life. It embodied, in their judgment, Communist tendencies which would destroy the federal system of government and the citizen's right to private property. Its enforcement would require the use of a massive federal force which would, in turn, destroy the sovereignty of the states and the freedom of the individual to choose his associates.

The vehemence of their convictions, together with a change in the course of American-Soviet relations, led the fundamentalists of the far right to reformulate their operations. Following the removal of Soviet weapons from Cuba and the increased hostility between Russia and China, the American public no longer showed sustained interest in the familiar radical right demands for "total victory" over the Reds. Most citizens refused to believe their nation was actually involved in World War III. To offset any decline in support, ultrafundamentalist leaders shifted the attention of their followers away from total victory and towards the new conspiracy, the "Moscow-led" civil rights movement.[24]

From the outset, all far rightists agreed that the 1963 Civil Rights Bill was pro-Moscow. Drs. McIntire and Hargis endorsed that view and contributed their own theologically oriented objections. They made clear they were not racist or anti-Negro. Hargis stated, "I knew it was wrong to deprive the Negroes of their constitutional rights. I'm criticized for this stand in the South." Dr. McIntire presented Negro spokesmen at his meetings. The schools identified with the Twentieth Century Reformation have admitted Negroes.

The two spoksmen, however, advocated somewhat divergent means to achieve the goal of equal justice. Dr. Hargis wrote that segregation is "one of Nature's universal laws. No intermingling or crossbreeding with animals of widely different characteristics takes place except under abnormal or artificial conditions. It is my conviction that God ordained segregation."[25]

[24] This was first suggested by David Danzig, "Rightists, Racists and Separatists," *Commentary* XXXVIII (Aug., 1964), 28-32.

[25] A Christian Crusade pamphlet, "The Truth About Segregation," pp. 1-2; John Kay Adams, "Saving America, Inc.," *The Nation*, Sept. 30, 1961, p. 195; Hargis also suggested that Christian Crusade establish segregated chapters for its members; "Echoes of the Convention: Sixth Annual Convention of Christian Crusade," p. 15. One student of Hargis states the crusader has "long since repudiated" the racist pamphlet, "The Truth About Segregation"; Redekop, *The American Far Right: A Case Study of Billy James Hargis and Christian*

In a 1958 convention, the ACCC approved a resolution: "Segregation within the church on racial, linguistic, and national lines is not unchristian nor contrary to the specific commands of the Bible." Leaders of the council's program for young people, the International Christian Youth, wrote, "God has made room in His Church for many views and practices of social organization with regard to race. And the Church, living as she does in the tide of history, reflects the racial distinctiveness as of the peoples of the earth." In another statement McIntire wrote, "Segregation or apartheid is not sin *per se*. . . . The love which Christians have for one another does not in itself demand an integrated church. Men can be brothers in Christ and still believe that it is better for their families that the children not have social intercourse which may lead to an intermarriage between the white and the black." In 1965, he criticized the General Assembly of the Presbyterian Church, U.S.A., for not rejecting "intermarriage between the Negro and the white." Dr. Hargis told a reporter, "The only feeling I've got [toward the Negro] is I do not believe in intermarriage between races." [26]

The two ultrafundamentalist leaders presented the same biblical arguments. The Scriptures have one and only one answer to the racial issue; that answer is not the doctrine of the Father-hood of God and the Brotherhood of Man. Dr. Hargis stated in 1961 that such a view was "hogwash." He wrote that "Brother-hood would crush Christianity and all religions by equalizing them." As early as 1945, Dr. McIntire had stated: "Jesus Christ repudiated the popular doctrine that is on the lips of thousands of preachers today—the universal Fatherhood of God. There is no such doctrine taught in the Bible. Neither does its corollary, the

Crusade, p. 184. However, in 1965 I wrote Christian Crusade asking for a sampling of its pamphlets on civil rights; I received "The Truth About Segregation" with others, so apparently Hargis wanted it kept in circulation. He once wrote a letter to the editor of *Life* stating, "You can't produce any writings of mine against the Negroes or any minority race"; February 28, 1964, p. 23; he apparently forgot this pamphlet.

[26] *Christian Beacon,* May 8, 1958, p. 5; July 2, 1964, p. 3; McIntire's monthly Newsletter, May 25, 1965, p. 1; McIntire, *Outside the Gate* (Collings-wood, N. J.: Christian Beacon Press, 1967), pp. 61, 62. In 1966 the general secretary of the ACCC was working to establish affiliated Negro churches in Philadelphia and Chicago; *Christianity Today,* Nov. 11, 1966, p. 179; Martin, "I Call on Billy James Hargis," *Christian Herald,* Feb. 1967, p. 21.

brotherhood of man, exist in the Bible." In his judgment, not all men are the "children of God. The Bible is very clear on this point." McIntire later expressly repudiated the Golden Rule (Matt. 7:12) as being relevant to civil rights legislation.[27]

The conclusions drawn from these principles were obvious. No person is a child of infinite worth in the eyes of the Creator until he has been converted. Only born-again Christians are worthy of the love of God. Not until a person receives that gift from God can his hopes to be treated as a full person on this earth be justified on biblical grounds. Those persons who are not born again do not deserve a better life. Thus, the unregenerated Negro or any other person has no infallible, inerrant source of truth (the Bible) on which to base his claim for full citizenship. Once he has been born again, he will know heaven is his destination and the cares of this world become insignificant.

The Bible also served the ultrafundamentalist in his opposition to the 1964 Civil Rights Act concerning Title II, public accommodations, and Title VII, fair employment practices. Dr. McIntire found the Scriptures taught that no government had the right to invade a person's business or private property by telling him whom he must serve, hire, or promote. The Eighth Commandment stated, "Thou shalt not steal." The two titles stole property the individual had earned by himself for his own use. McIntire spelled out his reason for opposing civil rights and open housing laws. Each was "an attack upon our property system and is a major endeavor to alter our social structure for the advancement of socialism. The road to socialism and Communism is the road we are now pursuing in the various undertakings and the massive propaganda."[28]

The Bible was also cited, somewhat indirectly, to justify the belief that the civil rights acts were unconstitutional because they violated "State's rights." Both Hargis and McIntire believe God had inspired the authors of the Constitution of 1787 in some

[27] *Newsweek*, Dec. 4, 1961, p. 18; a Christian Crusade pamphlet, "Brotherhood of Man . . . a Smoke Screen," pp. 3-4; Carl McIntire, *The Rise of the Tyrant: Controlled Economy vs. Private Enterprise*, p. 205; *The Death of a Church*, pp. 71-72; "The Bible versus Civil Rights," p. 1.

[28] "The Bible versus Civil Rights," pp. 1-4; *Christian Beacon*, Jan. 9, 1964, p. 6; April 9, 1964, p. 2; and March 9, 1967, p. 7. Christian Crusade expressed much the same sentiment in its 1964 Leadership School; see "Highlights, Third Annual Leadership School," p. 7.

direct fashion; the systems of federalism and of separation of powers written into that document reflected his will. These principles were being defended by several leaders, the most prominent being the governor of Alabama, George C. Wallace. In 1964, Christian Crusade named him as "Christian Patriot of the Year." The *Christian Beacon* wrote during his primary campaigns in three northern states that Wallace was a man who "puts his faith in God." The voters of Maryland were congratulated for giving him 43 percent of their total vote. Dr. McIntire wrote that the governor truly wanted equal rights for the Negro but believed Alabama, and each state, should accomplish that goal in its own way.[29]

Further biblical grounds for protest centered on criticizing the leadership of the National Council of Churches and Dr Martin Luther King. In ultrafundamentalist thought, the NCC spokesmen rejected the true biblical foundations of equality, thus making their objectives contrary to God's will. The NCC and King were encouraging the Negroes to vote, and that was mixing religion and politics. By ministering to the physical as well as the spiritual needs of minority peoples, the NCC was not placing its full emphasis on personal evangelism. By working alongside such groups as the NAACP and CORE, the National Council was cooperating with groups advocating secular goals. Any "civil disobedience" must be unequivocally and immediately rejected. Those clergymen from the North who helped demonstrate for civil rights must be judged against God's commandment to "come ye out and be separate and touch not the unclean thing." [30] Dr. McIntire warned that people "from behind the Iron Curtain" were planning to "go to Mississippi" to help the NCC and associated church groups working there. No people from the Iron Curtain did arrive, but that was not his point. In his judgment the NCC was sympathetic

[29] *Christian Crusade*, Sept., 1964, p. 9; *Christian Beacon*, Jan. 13, 1966, pp. 4, 8; a Twentieth Century Reformation publication, "The Truth About Mississippi," p. 7; "The Ten Commandments and Civil Rights," *passim;* Billy James Hargis, *Communist America—Must It Be?*, chap. 5; *Christian Beacon*, April 2, 1964, p. 1; April 9, 1964, p. 2; Jan. 12, 1967, p. 3; see pp. 000-000 on Governor Wallace.

[30] These views are found in most issues of *Christian Crusade* and *Christian Beacon* for 1964, 1965, and 1966; see also the ACCC Literature Item No. 86, "Civil Disobedience"; a convenient summary is in *Christian Beacon*, March 10, 1966, p. 3.

to the internal conspiracy. Dr. King received the full treatment. Not only was the Nobel Laureate, in Hargis' unforgettable words, "a stinking racial agitator," and friendly toward Moscow, but his theology was flabby and his behavior a threat to respectable society.[31]

The Church League of America did not directly attack the civil rights movement. It reprinted and circulated a thoughtful article by Lee E. Dirks of the *National Observer* entitled "Church Lobbyists Step Up Pressure." Mr. Kaub and the American Council of Christian Laymen were not active during the controversy in Congress due largely to his failing health. The ACCL materials already in print harmonized fully with the McIntire-Hargis position. One pamphlet, "The Fatherhood of God," rejected that doctrine since it "was hatched in hell and incubated in the hotbed of modernism." Kaub had already written that racial integration promoted "miscegenation and mongrelization," the NCC was "Communist controlled," and any church advocating desegregation was "soft on communism." The "Zionists" were "anxious to detroy the Nordic culture by forcing integration of white gentiles with the Negro race." [32]

The fundamentalists of the far right told the Negroes to take two specific steps. In convention the ACCC stated

> Christian Negroes are therefore called upon to repudiate clergymen of all races and reject their leadership if they refuse to accept the Bible as fully inspired, as authoritative; if they refuse to acknowledge the deity of Christ and the other doctrines of the historic Christian faith, and if such leadership agrees or cooperates with the program of the National Council of Churches.[33]

Dr. Hargis outlined a similar course. He pointed the Negro to

[81] The "agitator" quotation is in Donald Quinn, *The Oklahoma Courier*, reprinted in the U.S., Congress, Senate, *Congressional Record*, 87th Cong. 2nd sess., 1962, 108, pt. 5, 6579-80; see also the *Christian Beacon* for these issues: April 2, 1964, p. 1; Aug. 27, 1964, p. 6; Sept. 3, 1964, p. 8; Sept. 10, 1964, p. 1; Oct. 29, 1964, p. 7; and Nov. 5, 1964, pp. 4, 5, 8.
[82] See the ACCL promotional letter, "Challenge," vol. VII (May, 1959), *passim.*
[83] *Christian Beacon*, Nov. 5, 1964, p. 5; Hargis, *Communist America*, p. 109.

97

"The Old Rugged Cross." It is to this cross and to the resurrection of the Saviour of the world, Jesus Christ, that the Negro people must look, for only in the gospel may be found the 'truth' which 'shall make you free.' " [84]

In summary, what seemed beyond any doubt to ACCC–ICCC leaders during the Thousand Days was the fantastic increase in power by the internal conspirators. No other explanation could bring into focus the results of New Frontier liberalism, the *détente* with the Soviets, the decisions of the Supreme Court, the insidious appeal of the civil rights movement, and the whitewash by the Warren Commission. America was being tested; God had allowed all this to happen so true Christians would know what he expected of them. Though the times could hardly be more bleak, one must never despair. Perhaps through all this clamor and hatred God was telling America what it must do.

The fundamentalists of the far right found God was very close to them in 1964. He gave them more money, more supporters, more publicity, and more influence in public life than ever before. Above all, he gave them a cause—a cause so exciting, so challenging that it had to be providential; no other explanation would do. What did it matter that the cynics and scoffers and apostates called it "extremism," or "In your guts you know he's nuts." Yes, to be sure, the cause was centered on a person, but it was more than that. It was the reality that finally, right now, America had the chance to drive the traitors from the temple and reassert its rightful position as God's most favored nation. The cause was good, solid Christian Americanism, a return to the fundamentals. Now it was clear God was so generous in 1964; he wanted his people to use that money, publicity, and influence and to use it right away.

The rapid rise into prominence of Senator Barry Goldwater and its repurcussions in 1964 is a story too well known to be repeated here. What follows in this and the next chapter is an account of why the ultrafundamentalists supported him and how this led to their yielding most of their cherished separationist isola-

[84] *Christian Beacon,* Nov. 5, 1964, p. 5.

tion from other groups as they banded with the radical right to work for the cause.

During the early 1960's, Senator Goldwater had come to be recognized as the most consistent, articulate, and popular of the militant conservative Republican senators. He had freely supported Senator Joseph R. McCarthy, he had never received less than "99 percent" approval for his congressional voting record from the Americans for Constitutional Action (see below, pp. 113-14) and in 1960, he had been the presidential candidate of both the editors of *National Review* and of the John Birch Society.

Across the nation he was the most sought-after speaker at the rallies of the budding far right groups. At a convention of We, the People! in Chicago, he, along with Hargis and Revilo P. Oliver, attacked the liberals, finding them controlled by the internal conspiracy. The senator pointed out the presence of Communists in the fields of textbook and Sunday school curriculum writing; he found Communists in radio and television, the cinema, the Army, Navy, Diplomatic Corps, Civil Service, Treasury Department, "and other control points of government." [35] His address was standard fare for a radical right meeting, but he was not just one more speaker. He was offering the audience the power and prestige of his office as a United States senator. His followers on the far right used this endorsement as proof they were the true conservatives in this country fighting for American liberty.

Throughout the early 1960's the ultrafundamentalists expressed their enthusiasm for Senator Goldwater with great caution. They knew their tax-exempt status with the Internal Revenue Service would be jeopardized by any form of political endorsement. A careful reader could detect no overt support for the Arizonian in the publications of the Twentieth Century Reformation, the ACCC-ICCC, or the Church League of America.

Dr. Hargis pursued another course. The delegates to the annual Christian Crusade convention in August, 1963, willingly told reporters they favored Goldwater. During the roll call of states

[35] A Christian Crusade pamphlet, "Counter Strategy for Counter Attack," pp. 3-4; at the same meeting Professor Oliver told the delegates they could find Communists "in their clubs, their schools, their churches and their courts"; Joseph Gusfield, *Symbolic Crusade: Status Politics and the American Temperance Movement* (Urbana: University of Illinois Press, 1963), p. 181.

only the word "Arizona" drew applause. The Crusaders loudly cheered the attacks of Edwin A. Walker on the presidential hopes of Richard Nixon, Nelson Rockefeller, and George Romney. The name of Goldwater was not mentioned during the formal proceedings of the convention. The delegates could draw their own conclusions as to Crusade support, when they looked up to the balcony wall of the convention hall and there found a very large photograph of Senator Goldwater.[36]

By the time the Republicans met in San Francisco for the nominating convention, the conservatives had already completed their work. The great majority of delegates were already committed to Goldwater. His appeal, in James Reston's words, was "not intellectual, but emotional; rugged, outspoken, a dukes-up fighter against Washington, Wall Street, Eastern domination, Communism, foreign aid, and everything that is in Republican eyes 'soft' and ambiguously confusing." [37]

The climactic moment in the brief history of the radical right appeared during the senator's acceptance speech.

> Now my fellow Americans, the tide has been running against freedom. Our people have followed false prophets. We must, and we shall, return to proven ways—not because they are old, but because they are true.
>
> Anyone who joins us in all sincerity we welcome. Those, who do not care for our cause, we don't expect to enter our ranks in any case. And let our Republicanism so focused and so dedicated not be made fuzzy and futile by unthinking and stupid labels.
>
> I would remind you that extremism in the defense of liberty is no vice! And let me remind you also that moderation in the pursuit of justice is no virtue! [38]

A titanic surge of cheering burst over the Cow Palace. Delegates stood on their chairs shouting and clapping. To the radical right, the magical words had been spoken; politics had been transformed into religion. The endorsement of "extremism" in its un-

[36] *New York Times,* Aug. 5, 1963, p. 15; *The Christian Century,* Aug. 21, 1963, p. 1039.
[37] *New York Times,* July 3, 1964, p. 17.
[38] *New York Times,* July 17, 1964, p. 10.

qualified simplicity was tantamount to an endorsement of the kind of patriotism consonant with the far right. The nominee of a major party, a senator for twelve years, had rebuffed the king-makers' strongest attacks. He had proved he would not compromise with principle. In the full context of convention proceedings, and with the television cameras at that moment showing former Vice-President Richard Nixon making no cheers or applause, the radical right across the nation had achieved political power.[39]

[39] *Ibid.*, pp. 10, 17; an editorial in *National Review*, Sept. 8, 1964, p. 756; George B. Leonard, "What is an Extremist?", *Look*, Oct. 20, 1964, p. 33. Two penetrating assessments of the transformation of politics into religion are William Stringfellow, *Dissenter in a Great Society* (New York: Holt, Rinehart & Winston, 1966), pp. 57-66, and Lester DeKoster, "I'm an Extremist, But . . . ," *The Reformed Journal*, Sept., 1964, pp. 3-4.

5
The Loss of Identity, 1964

From the moment the Republican presidential nominee finished his acceptance speech, Americans sought to understand the meaning of Senator Goldwater's nomination. Was this compaign going to produce a real choice and not just an echo? Would it spark a genuine conservative-liberal dialogue? Were the millions of disgruntled voters still smarting from the defeat of Senator Robert Taft in 1952 going to vote in 1964? Was America really moving back from the left to the right? These were logical, valid questions and the general public took them up with the sobriety they deserved.

In the ranks of the fundamentalists of the far right, however, no one called for a dialogue. Dr. Hargis expressed the sentiments of the group when in July he stated that Goldwater's nomination was "one of God's blessings to Christian Conservatives." He found it showed "God has been working on the side of Christian Conservatives the last eight months." The GOP platform, he pointed out, "is the greatest thing given us in my lifetime." A month later he proclaimed the election of Goldwater in November "would be the millennium." At their August convention, Christian Crusaders awarded *in absentia* their "Man of the Year" Award to Senator Goldwater.[1]

The unanimous support given the Arizona senator by the entire far right was the result of a long series of events first begun in the late 1950's. As seen above, the radical right and the ultra-fundamentalists began at that time to share a common political ideology, but had achieved no organic unity because the latter remained suspicious of everyone outside their own ranks. This chapter surveys the increasing amount of cooperation between these two groups; it attempts to show how their common interest in "Christian Conservatism" brought them into a working partnership by November, 1964, and what this outreach meant for those whose identity had rested so long on the practice of total separation.

The programs and ideologies of the radical right and the ultrafundamentalists interlocked at many points during the early 1960's. Although no precise means of measurement exist, the trend towards increasing cooperation became evident in at least four areas: sources of information, action programs, celebrities, and endorsements.

The far right and the ACCC–ICCC devoted a substantial portion of their programs to documenting the operations of the internal conspiracy. The spokesmen were convinced their indictment was faultless because it rested on facts, unassailable facts. Knowing their followers lacked the time and resources to gather this information for themselves, the leaders in both factions presented themselves to the public as guides to understanding the crisis of the times.

Dr. Hargis advertised one of his early studies as containing:

[1] Hargis did not forget the internal conspiracy. He characterized the *Denver Post*, which was critical of his crusade, as "the worst newspaper in America . . . the most evil influence in the world." To him it was "so left wing . . . so Socialist I don't know why Khrushchev would object to the sale of this paper on the streets of Moscow," *Denver Post*, July 20, 1964, p. 11; *New York Times*, Aug. 9, 1964, p. 55; see the pamphlet "Echoes of the Convention: Sixth Annual National Convention of Christian Crusade" (Tulsa, 1964), pp. 3-5; *Christian Crusade*, Sept., 1964, pp. 8-9.

Read pure, unadulterated Anti-communist FACT—as never before presented! Unmistakable! Dynamic! [2]

The general far right and the ultrafundamentalists started to interlock in the realm of their educational activities by utilizing the same sources of information. This led, almost inevitably, to the appearance of a unified interpretation of the internal conspiracy by each of the participating factions. One could find, for instance, the Twentieth Century Reformation publications making the same kind of judgment on the income tax or fluoridation of water as did the John Birch Society or We, the People!

Each national office of the ACCC–ICCC and the radical right drew its facts from four general sources of information. Each maintained its own office records, clippings, and raw data. Each used the same state and national government publications. Each accepted as definitive several widely circulated secondary interpretations of the conspiracy within. Finally, each used publications furnished them by professional suppliers.

The first source, the office records, consisted of extensive clippings from local and regional newspapers and journals sent to the national headquarters by supporters. These data contained reports on speeches made or meetings attended or resolutions adopted by those known or suspected of belonging to the internal conspiracy. This information was of enormous value to the leaders since it was rarely published by the national news media. To aid their readers even more, the ultrafundamentalists often reprinted complete articles in their publications they had received from followers. [3]

Each office also maintained its own extensive files on suspected individuals and programs. This information was sold on request to inquirers who were informed to consider their contributors as tax-deductible gifts to religious enterprises. The data were drawn from clippings, from published governmental reports, and from the materials originally collected by such contributors as

[2] The statement on the back cover of his book, *Communism—The Total Lie* (Tulsa: Christian Crusade Press, 1963).

[3] See, for example, the report on Bishop James Pike at Harlingen, Texas, in the *Christian Beacon,* Jan. 21, 1965, pp. 2, 3; the Hargis Newsletter, March 15, 1964, p. 1.

J. B. Matthews and Allan Zoll, both of whom associated with Verne P. Kaub. The Matthews collection was given to the Church League of America and Dr. Hargis purchased the Zoll records. These files also contained most of the publications of all other far right organizations, and these were frequently cited as authoritative sources of information. Dr. Hargis explained how the files were used.

> When we find a minister whose name is signed to such left-wing ads in *The New York Times,* as "Bring Red China into the U. N." or "Get Out of South Viet Nam," we note that on a card. Then we tuck that card away in our files. Pretty soon this establishes a pattern because real left wingers don't sign one petition. They sign others.[4]

Additional facts were gleaned from governmental publications dealing with communism. The most widely used items came from the House Un-American Activities Committee and the Senate Internal Security Committee along with the Attorney General's list of subversive organizations. These were utilized most frequently when individuals under suspicion were linked with the internal conspiracy through the listing of their membership in Communist front and alleged front groups. Although severely criticized for many years, this procedure was used by the ultra-fundamentalists and the far right to establish an aura of official governmental verification for their indictments.[5]

[4] Pete Martin, "I Call on Billy James Hargis," *Christian Herald,* Feb., 1967, p. 77; "Price List of the Church League of America," pp. 6-7; Harry and Bonaro Overstreet, *The Strange Tactics of Extremism* (New York: W. W. Norton, 1964), pp. 198 99; *St. Louis Post-Dispatch,* Feb. 27, 1962. For more information on Zoll, see the many references in Raywid, *The Ax-Grinders;* Arnold Forster and Benjamin R. Epstein, *The Troublemakers* (Garden City, N, Y., Doubleday & Co., 1952), pp. 207-8, 212-13; Jack Nelson and Gene Roberts, Jr., *The Censors and the Schools* (Boston: Little, Brown, 1963), pp. 46-49.

[5] The following are excellent analyses of this kind of documentation: Philip Wogaman, "The Methodist Ministry and Communism: The Truth Behind the Charges," a pamphlet of The Methodist Church (n.d.); Gordon L. Shull, "Communism and Anti-Communism in America: The Long Road to Reason," *Social Progress* XVI (Nov.-Dec., 1965), pp. 11-30; John F. Cronin, "Anti-Communism and Freedom," *America* (April 22, 1961, pp. 172-74; Julian Foster, "None Dare Call It Reason: A Critique of John Stormer's *None Dare Call It Treason*" (published by the author, Fullerton, California, 1964); Keith R. Sanders, "An Empirical Study of the Integrity of Evidence Used in John A. Stormer's *None Dare Call It Treason*" (Ph.D. diss., Pittsburgh University, 1969).

THE POLITICS OF DOOMSDAY

A third source of information shared by all factions were the several widely read secondary interpretations which came to be accepted as irrefutable fact. The best known works were: Edgar C. Bundy, *Collectivism in the Churches;* John Flynn, *The Road Ahead;* Billy James Hargis, *Communist America—Must It Be?;* Verne P. Kaub, *Collectivism Challenges Christianity;* Carl Mc-Intire; *Author of Liberty;* E. Merrill Root, *Brainwashing in the High Schools;* Fred C. Schwarz, *You Can Trust the Communists to Be Communists;* John Stormer, *None Dare Call It Treason;* and Robert Welch, *The Blue Book* and *The Politician.* Pamphlets, articles, tracts, and other printed matter published by the radical right and the ACCC–ICCC leaders often cited one or more of these titles as being so authoritative as to preclude the need for further documentation.

Two shorter works were also widely used. A perennial favorite was the tract, "How Red Is the National Council of Churches?" It was later revised by Dr. Donald A. Waite, an occasional associate of Dr. McIntire. The new edition did not show evidence of having considered the many refutations made of its original charges. The second item was a pamphlet, the 1958 report of the "Special Committee on Communist Tactics, Strategy, and Objectives of the American Bar Association," printed in the *Congressional Record* on August 22, 1958, and again on March 1, 1962.[6]

The fourth source of common information was the material furnished by professional suppliers, such as the National Education Program of Searcy, Arkansas, and the Circuit Riders of Cincinnati, Ohio. While no formal organizational ties exist between these and the ultrafundamentalists, the latter publish extensively from their wide variety of offerings. Of perennial interest has been the NEP best-seller film, "Communism on the Map." Lowman produced several long lists of "Certain Activities of . . ." various church and public officials which he found un-American. His booklets became best sellers among the ultrafundamentalists.[7]

[6] This was not an official report by the Association which later published a more subdued version in its journal; Ralph E. Ellsworth and Sarah M. Harris, *The American Right Wing* (Washington: Public Affairs Press, 1962), pp. 24-25 and note 69, p. 57.

[7] A well-known writer for NEP is Dr. James Bales who frequently contributed to *Christian Crusade;* George Thayer, *The Farther Shores of Politics: The*

A few suppliers concentrated on distribution of materials produced by others. By subscribing to their services the national offices of the ACCC–ICCC leaders could keep in touch with the full spectrum of far right publications. One of the most representative of these was the Network of Patriotic Letter Writers in California, "united to preserve America's precious heritage." It offered very low-priced reprints of articles and documents which, its directors stated, had been "often repressed under managed news policies." Opinion makers such as McIntire, Hargis, or Bundy, or anyone else could purchase a study, for example, proving both Karl Marx and the American government favored free public education. Dr. McIntire's pamphlet "UNICEF and the Reds" sold for $0.03. For a penny less a customer could purchase "How Far to the Left Is the League of Women Voters?" For the same price he could also find how "The Crisis in Our Girl Scout Movement" had been exposed. The standard fare, however, centered on the usual topics: the income tax, disarmament, the PTA, the Supreme Court, Bishop James Pike, urban renewal, mental health, and the National and World Councils of Churches.[8]

The ultrafundamentalists also moved towards greater cooperation with the radical right. Several speakers appeared often in both ACCC–ICCC and far right circles. The best known of these were: Edwin A. Walker, John Stormer, J. B. Matthews, and Dr. E. Merrill Root.

Mr. Walker became a regular lecturer at Christian Crusade and John Birch Society meetings. He also was engaged as the annual Labor Day weekend speaker at the Christian Admiral Hotel, the summer headquarters of the Twentieth Century Reformation and the American-International Councils of Christian Churches. His appearance there was unique in that he and Senator Strom Thurmond of South Carolina were by 1964 the only sched-

---

American Political Fringe Today (New York: Simon and Schuster, 1967), pp. 272-78; Donald Janson and Bernard Eismann, *The Far Right*, chap. 6; Harry and Bonaro Overstreet, *The Strange Tactics of Extremism*, pp. 157-59, 301; Nelson and Roberts, *The Censors and the Schools*, pp. 90-91, 153-54; Robert Welch, *The Politician* (published by the author, Belmont, 1963) pp. lxxxiii-iv; the reply of The Methodist Church to Lowman is found in the Wogaman pamphlet cited in note 5 of this chapter.

[8] See the mimeographed cover letter in their introductory packet and the Newsletter of June, 1965.

uled lecturers at the McIntire center who were not in some immediate manner members of denominations belonging to the ACCC or the ICCC. These two spokesmen, in other words, were nonseparationists addressing those who prided themselves on their unique identity as separationists. Walker also spoke on the Hargis and McIntire radio broadcasts and frequently addressed such meetings as the Congress of Conservatives and the New England Rally for God and Country. It should be noted that his appearance at the Christian Admiral did not mean that the ACCC–ICCC leaders necessarily endorsed all of his ideas. He attracted considerable attention by stating over national television, "I'll bet you will find more good Americans in the Ku Klux Klan than in the A.D.A." [Americans for Democratic Action.] The *Christian Beacon,* Hargis, and Bundy have expressly repudiated the Ku Klux Klan.[9]

A second personality who bridged the gap between the far right and the ultrafundamentalists was John Stormer, author and publisher of *None Dare Call It Treason.* The book, an instant success with the radical right, was considered the most accurate indictment in print of the internal conspiracy. Stormer himself became active in ACCC–ICCC circles, serving on several standing committees and accompanying McIntire on overseas tours. His writings showed how clearly he understood the homogeneity within the full radical right movement. He suggested that his readers study *Human Events, The Wanderer, Dan Smoot Report,* the *Christian Beacon,* and *Christian Economics,* all of which had some direct tie to his cause. He commended the American Legion, the Daughters of the American Revolution, the John Birch Society, the Cardinal Mindzenty Foundation, and the Christian Anti-Communism Crusade. In his book he singled out for special praise the broadcasts of Hargis and McIntire and gave the mailing addresses of the ultrafundamentalist offices alongside those of America's Future, the Circuit Riders, Americans for Constitutional Action, Young Americans for Freedom, and the Foundation for Economic

[9] As quoted in *Common Sense,* Nov. 15, 1965, p. 3; *Christian Beacon,* July 30, 1964, p. 8; in July, 1965, Walker addressed a rally of the group, "We, The White People" at the state capitol of Louisiana; Minneapolis *Star,* July 5, 1965, p. 4B.

Education.[10] In brief, Stormer moved to work with those who had not necessarily taken a stand for pure doctrine.

A third celebrity who commanded enormous respect in all camps of the radical right was J. B. Matthews. His entry into the movement has already been described in chapter 3. In the early 1960's, he became a major contributor of articles, speeches, and pamphlets to a wide variety of anticommunist groups. He spoke at both Christian Crusade and Twentieth Century Reformation rallies; he made tapes and wrote articles for the Church League of America and its journal, *News and Views*. His works were sold by Kaub's League. He was, in short, one of the few individuals engaged by every major ultrafundamentalist enterprise. He also published frequently in *The Independent American* (the journal of Kent and Phoebe Courtney), the organs of the John Birch Society, and in America's Future, an organization devoted to assessing public school textbooks.[11]

In their enthusiasm for the far right crusade, the ultrafundamentalists embraced individuals whose own doctrine was far removed from their theology. The best known example of this trend was the professor emeritus of English at Earlham College, Dr. E. Merrill Root. A lifelong Quaker, Root found little opportunity within ACCC–ICCC circles to express his doctrinal convictions. However, the ultrafundamentalists recognized him as an expert on the workings of the internal conspiracy in education. His two major books, both outside his academic specialty, were *Collectivism on the Campus* and *Brainwashing in the High Schools*. He became an endorser of the John Birch Society and member of We, the People!, the Congress of Freedom, and a contributor to *The Freeman* and *Human Events*. Dr. Root was judged by friends

---

[10] *The Independent American*, May-June, 1965, p. 8; *Christian Beacon*, Aug. 19, 1965, p. 1; John Stormer, "Anatomy of a Smear" (Florissant, Missouri: Liberty Bell Press, 1965); *passim; Christian Beacon*, March 24, 1966, p. 4; Nov. 4, 1965, pp. 1, 8; *None Dare Call It Treason*, chap. 14.

[11] Church League, "Price List," pp. 18, 21, 22, 30; see the Courtney's "Tax Fax No. 31, Communist Infiltration in Religion"; J. Alln Broyles, *The John Birch Society: Anatomy of a Protest* (Boston: Beacon Press, 1964), p. 41; Robert Welch, *The Blue Book*, 5th ed., pp. 160-61; Raywid, *The Ax-Grinders*, chap. 8, especially pp. 128, 146-48; Nelson and Roberts, *The Censors and the Schools*, chap. 6; Jack Anderson and Ronald W. May, *McCarthy: The Man, The Senate, The 'Ism'* (Boston: Beacon Press, 1952), pp. 313, 344.

and critics as having "more influence than any other man in the attempts of pressure groups to rewrite American textbooks." [12] His books were sold by all ACCC–ICCC outlets. More to the point, he participated directly as a nonseparationist in several formal programs of the ultrafundamentalists. He wrote articles and made tapes for the Church League; in 1962 he joined McIntire in speaking at the dedication of the new headquarters of the Church League.

Although some rivalry for membership and contributions existed among the many radical right groups, some individual members of the ACCC–ICCC joined organizations with competing interests. This, in turn, helped bring more ultrafundamentalists into the orbit of the far right. Throughout the early 1960's two individuals especially reflected this dual allegiance: Milton M. Lory and Dr. George J. Hess.

Mr. Lory served on the board of trustees of Shelton College of which McIntire was chairman and later president. He spoke often at the Christian Admiral Hotel summer meetings. He also addressed rallies of Christian Crusade and served on its board of advisors, one of the few individuals to circulate in both the Hargis and McIntire camps. At the same time he joined We, the People!, Freedom Forum, the Congress of Freedom, Wake Up America Committee, the Liberty Amendment Committee, and the American Coalition of Patriotic Societies. [18]

Dr. Hess, of Bunker Hill, Illinois, served as president of the Association of American Physicians and Surgeons and a member of the Committee of Endorsers of the John Birch Society and the advisory board of Christian Crusade and the Conservative Society

[12] Nelson and Roberts, *The Censors and the Schools*, p. 55; see here also chap. 4, for comments by Root on such issues as the Birch Society, fluoridation, mental health programs, and Quakers; Raywid, *The Ax-Grinders*, pp. 136-39; Church League, "Price List," pp. 19, 25, 33; he wrote "Tax Fax no. 37, Subversion in the Schools" for the Courtneys.

[18] *Christian Beacon*, March 19, 1964, p. 4; June 17, 1965, p. 1; Feb. 6, 1964, p. 1; *Christian Crusade*, Nov., 1964, p. 25; his views on education are in Raywid, *The Ax-Grinders*, pp. 12, 20; *The Independent American*, March-April, 1965, p. 5; *The Greater Nebraskan* (Omaha), Summer, 1965, p. 2. The bi-monthly newsletter of the American Coalition in which he is a leader, carries articles and reprints reflecting the far right view on UNICEF, Secretary McNamara, antipoverty legislation, Vietnam, the Federal Communications Commission, foreign policy, and civil rights; *Christian Crusade*, March, 1965, p. 5.

of America. He was active in the Congress of Conservatives and the Wake Up America Committee. As an active layman in the Independent Fundamental Baptist Church, he learned of the programs of the American Council of Christian Churches and joined its Laymen's Commission. This latter is the body that absorbed Kaub's council in 1964. Dr. Hess also addressed Christian Crusade meetings.[14]

Along with mutual sources of information, shared action programs, and interlocking celebrities, the ultrafundamentalists moved out of the isolationism in the early 1960's by endorsing or showing strong approval of several well-known radical right crusades. An important qualification must be made at this point. Dr. Hargis consistently made known his great enthusiasm for a large number of far right groups. Mr. Kaub also worked actively in many anticommunist programs. However, neither of these men had chosen to adhere as closely to the dictates of total separation as had McIntire and Bundy. The latter two made explicit the fact that none of the programs with which they were associated were in any manner organically or constitutionally interlocked with any other organization; this included the Twentieth Century Reformation, the *Christian Beacon*, the American and International Councils of Christian Churches, and the Church League of America.

Bundy stated that the Church League of America had "absolutely no connection with the John Birch Society." [15] However, a brochure published in 1962 by the John Birch Society lists on its Committee of Endorsers the name of Mr. E. L. Wiegand. He was also listed in the Church League's "Price List" as a member of the board of directors of the Church League of America.[16] The December, 1965, issue of *American Opinion*, the organ of the John Birch Society, carried a paid advertisement for a 1965 publication of the Church League of America entitled, "The Record

[14] A 1962 one-page brochure of the John Birch Society; a mimeographed, undated letter of the Laymen's Commission, American Council of Christian Churches; *The Independent American*, March-April, 1965, p. 3; *Free Enterprise* (published by We, The People!, Chicago), Jan., 1965, p. 8; *Focus/Midwest 64* vol. III (St. Louis, Missouri), entitled "Roster of the Right Wing in Illinois and Missouri," p. 18.
[15] *News and Views*, March, 1965, p. 7.
[16] "Price List," p. 12; see also Group Research, Inc., "Finances of the Right Wing," p. 13; Anti-Defamation League, *Facts*, Nov.-Dec., 1961, p. 228.

of the NCCC." In the revised edition of *The Politician*, Mr. Welch cited the publications of Bundy and Matthews as being authoritative.[17]

Neither McIntire nor Bundy has been or is a member of the John Birch Society. In public statements McIntire has defended Robert Welch. In 1961 he wrote, "But the leader of the John Birch Society never called President Eisenhower a Communist as reported in the newspapers." Again, in 1965, after Senator Frank Church of Idaho had pointed in the January 26 issue of *Look* to the internal-conspiracy thesis in Welch's writings, McIntire stated that Welch had never stated President Eisenhower was "consciously serving the Communist conspiracy." McIntire said Welch's statements were taken out of context; the Communist-inspired motivation of Eisenhower's foreign policy was only one of several possibilities Welch was offering by way of explaining the record of American foreign policy in the years 1953 to 1961.

However, it should be noted Dr. McIntire was referring to later editions of *The Politician* in which Welch had softened his earlier charges against President Eisenhower. An early edition of that book stated, "My firm conviction that Dwight Eisenhower is a dedicated, conscious agent of the Communist conspiracy is based on an accumulation of detailed evidence so extensive and so palpable that it seems to me to put this conviction beyond any reasonable doubt." [18] McIntire apparently had overlooked that conclusion.

Other ACCC statements point to the approval by the ultra-fundamentalists of the John Birch Society. Its youth organization, International Christian Youth, published a pamphlet, "Christian Extremism and the UN." The writer criticized a "Mr. Novak" television program for having its anti-UN spokesman appear to be a fool, if not mentally ill, for stating, "I can be sure, if I'm on God's side." The writer added that the answers to life's problems were already known to those "rightly interpreting" the Word of

[17] *News and Views,* March, 1964, p. 1; Welch, *The Politician* (1963 ed.), pp. lxxxiv, 84-86, 223, note 4.
[18] Broyles, *The John Birch Society,* pp. 7, 162; Broyles also traces the modifications made in the later editions of *The Politician; Christian Beacon,* May 25, 1961, p. 4; Jan. 28, 1965, p. 4.

God, and then he added, " 'Psychopathic' Christian still believe it's wrong to do business with anyone who refuses to recognize any particular standard as *the* Word of God. They're the kind who join the John Birch Society."

One of the rooms refurnished by voluntary contributions at the Christian Admiral Hotel was named "The John Birch Room." One letter to McIntire in the *Christian Beacon* is perhaps representative of a broad sector of reader opinion: "It was through the J.B.S. I became interested in you and your program. I constantly try to recruit new listeners for your program, as time is running out for us, and only if we awaken the people in time will we have a chance to save this beloved country of ours." [19]

Another far right group, Americans for Constitutional Action, has received support from the ultrafundamentalists. Two of its board members, General Bonner Fellers (retired) and Mr. Fred Koch, were also members of the advisory board of Christian Crusade. The *Christian Beacon* made known its opinion of ACA. When asked by a reader as to its judgment of certain congressmen, the managing editor wrote,

> We keep no "approved" list for reference in answering such questions, but we might refer you to the voting records of Congressmen kept by the Americans for Constitutional Action, an organization which does grade Congressmen according to their voting for and against safeguarding our Constitutional heritage.[20]

[19] *Christian Beacon,* Oct. 1, 1964, p. 2; the "UN" pamphlet is available from the Collingswood, New Jersey office; *Christian Beacon,* March 24, 1966, p. 4; March 2, 1967, p. 5; the letter of the editor is in Nov. 26, 1964, issue, p. 4; a penetrating criticism is Lester DeKoster, "The Christian and the John Birch Society" (Grand Rapids: Eerdmans Publishing Company, 1966), a pamphlet. McIntire's associate, Dr. Donald Waite, worked for several months as an assistant to Robert Welch at the Belmont, Massachusetts office; Welch understood how closely his movement paralleled that of ultrafundamentalism. He stated that although none of the groups the John Birch Society endorsed was "affiliated with us in any way," he fully approved the Twentieth Century Reformation, Christian Crusade, the Church League of America, and the American Council of Christian Laymen; as reported in the *Twelfth Report, Un-American Activities Committee in California, Report of the Senate Fact-Finding Committee on Un-American Activities to the 1963 Regular California Legislature* (Sacramento, 1963), pp. 20-21.

[20] *Christian Beacon,* Oct. 1, 1964, p. 2; Thayer, *The Farther Shores of Politics,* pp. 162-66; Arnold Forster and Benjamin R. Epstein, *Danger on the Right,* chap. 12.

Dr. McIntire also expressed his views on the Minutemen. Referring to the charge by Senator Frank Church in *Look* (January 26, 1965) that the group seriously threatened traditional American liberties, McIntire stated:

One of the surest proofs that there is no Right Wing conspiracy is that many of the names used in this attack are of people of whom we have no knowledge whatsoever. In reference to the Minutemen, and his [Senator Church's] discussion of them, we would remind the Senator from Idaho that there is an amendment to the Constitution which reads as follows, "A well-regulated militia being necessary to the security of a free state, the right of the people to keep and bear arms shall not be infringed" (Amendment II). Yes indeed, every home, every man, has a right to have arms that he may defend himself, and these maneuvers and suggestions that are being made now that all must be licensed is only an effort on the part of those who control, who are indeed the liberals, to find out who does and who does not have a gun in his house. And this is in violation of the protection which an individual is entitled to under the Constitution of the United States.[21]

In summary, during the early 1960's, prior to the nomination of Senator Goldwater for president, the ultrafundamentalists showed a growing willingness to forsake their separationism to work directly with those who shared their political convictions. That in itself was a momentous event for them. However, as the balance of this chapter will show, their enthusiasm for the Republican national ticket would draw them out even further to where by election day they would be virtually indistinguishable from their nonseparationist brothers.

After the formal opening of the 1964 campaign on Labor Day, the fundamentalists of the far right started a slow paced, cautious program of letting their supporters know where they

[21] *Christian Beacon,* Jan. 28, 1965, p. 5.

stood on the candidates and the issues but without making a formal endorsement. The danger of losing tax-exempt status prevented any overt sign of approval. Hargis and Schwarz explained that although their crusades "will not officially endorse a presidential candidate, they are throwing their personal support to Senator Barry Goldwater." [22] The *Christian Beacon* printed comments approving many of the positions taken by the GOP national ticket. Bundy did not make a public statement of preference. The *News and Views,* which he edited, published proconservative items during the camgaign months, climaxed by offering for rent or sale a twenty-eight-minute film, "How the Communists and Religious Liberals Hate Barry Goldwater!" The script was later printed as a *News and Views* issue and the film was kept in circulation after the election. [23]

The fourth ultrafundamentalist leader, Verne Kaub, was in failing health during the summer months and died in September. The American Council of Christian Laymen as such was not active during the campaign. An associate of Kaub, Allan A Zoll, turned up on a Citizens for Goldwater-Miller payroll in mid-September. The St. Louis *Post-Dispatch* reported that Zoll attempted to uncover further activities of Walter Jenkins of the White House staff, and was understood to have kept in touch with H. L. Hunt, banker of the right-wing Life Lines program. [24]

Neither Senator Goldwater nor Representative Miller made any special appeal to the ultrafundamentalists as such. If anything, the religious affiliation of the two leaders should have led the ACCC–ICCC to restate its traditional hostility towards Roman Catholicism, which would include Miller, and Episcopalianism, which would include Goldwater. In 1960, the *Christian Beacon* had made its position perfectly clear in regard to Roman Catholicism (see p. 118-19). The Protestant Episcopal Church, to which Goldwater belonged, was a full member of the National

[22] A news item in *The Christian Century,* Oct. 7, 1964, p. 1254.

[23] See pp. 118-19 for the specific response of the *Beacon;* the script of the movie is *News and Views,* Nov., 1964; the Church League did not produce a comparable film on how the religious conservatives hated Lyndon Johnson. I viewed its Goldwater film at the River-Lake Tabernacle, Minneapolis, in December, 1964.

[24] See a series of articles collected in pamphlet form, "Ultraconservatism in the 1964 Presidential Election," *St. Louis Post-Dispatch,* Dec., 1964, p. 7.

and World Councils of Churches. To the ACCC–ICCC those councils were filled with apostates, social gospelers, one-worlders, modernists, liberals, and what-have-you doing the work of Satan. The religious affiliations of the national Republican ticket were those which had been flatly repudiated by the fundamentalists of the far right.

During the campaign, Senator Goldwater carefully avoided what he called "organ-tone windups" and public demonstrations of personal piety. His own personal creed, as published in August, fell far short of the standards for doctrinal purity demanded by all fundamentalists. For instance, he stated his busy schedule frequently made it difficult to attend church regularly. He told reporters,

> If a man acts in a religious way, an ethical way, then he's really a religious man—and it doesn't have a lot to do with how often he gets inside a church.
>
> With me it is like old Senator Henry Ashurst of Arizona used to say: "The saddle is my church, and the trees are my catehdral." I get a lot of the same feeling from going up the canyons or walking in the desert.[25]

Although he understood conservative theology (he once underlined all the passages in an Episcopal prayerbook which religious conservatives could accept), he spoke only in general terms about "Divine Will" or God. He had written his twelve-year-old daughter, "Smile, think right, believe in God, your family, and your country." To a son he wrote, "There is no foundation like the rock of honesty and fairness, and when you begin to build your life on that rock with the cement of the faith in God that you have, then, brother, you have a real start." [26] Although ultra-fundamentalists traditionally had been sharply critical of so complete an emphasis on ethics as compared to propositional theology, they made no comment on this aspect of the senator's convictions.

It was clear the theological position of President Johnson also failed to harmonize with ACCC–ICCC standards. Thus, the fundamentalists of the far right turned to other criteria by which to

[25] *Time*, Aug. 28, 1964, p. 56.
[26] *Ibid.*

116

THE LOSS OF IDENTITY, 1964

evaluate the candidates. Undoubtedly the issue which influenced their commitment more than any other was the Republican endorsement of the Becker Amendment to allow religious exercises in the public schools. Leaders and members of the ACCC–ICCC considered this issue of the highest possible priority. Senator Goldwater demanded that America no longer "ban Almighty God from our school rooms." The Twentieth Century Reformation reprinted and distributed most of his speech in a pamphlet, with this addition:

How the Parties Stand on a Bible-Prayer Amendment [27]

Barry M. Goldwater	*Lyndon B. Johnson*
-Strongly favors	-Silent
-Introduced an amendment	-Johnson Congress stalled all amendments

William E. Miller	*Hubert Humphrey*
-Strongly favors	-Opposes
-Signed Discharge Petition	-Condemns prayers in school

Republican Platform	*Democratic Platform*
-Urges passage	-Refuses to support
-Pledges support	

The journal of the new evangelicalism, *Christianity Today*, summarized the "religious issues" of the campaign. It believed the more moderate and liberal church elements would oppose Goldwater for three reasons: his vote against the Civil Rights Act, which most Protestant leaders had endorsed; the refusal of the national GOP ticket "to renounce the right-wing extremists who are a thorn in the flesh of liberal Protestantism and the ecumenical movement"; and Goldwater's support for the Becker Amendment because "virtually all major Protestant denominations have registered their opposition to such an amendment." [28] In each category

[27] See the Twentieth Century Reformation pamphlet "Barry Asks Prayer Amendment," which includes a reprint of a news story in the Newark *Sunday Times*, Oct. 11, 1964; see the *Christian Beacon*, July 16, 1964, pp. 5, 8, which points out the "close similarity" between the wording of the ACCC and the Republican Party statements on this issue.

[28] An editorial, "GOP Ticket: The Religious Factors," July 31, 1964, p. 1021. *Christianity Today* was hardly enthusiastic toward the Johnson administra-

117

the ultrafundamentalists would have reason to oppose the moderate-liberal camp; they too opposed the Civil Rights Act, they too considered the "right-wing extremist" label to be an unfair description of them, and they too supported a prayer-Bible amendment.

As the campaign wore on, the *Christian Beacon* moved more directly toward approval of Goldwater. The managing editor made a comparison between the Young Americans for Freedom, the ardently pro-Goldwater youth group, and the young people's organization of the ACCC–ICCC. He added, "Both produce the same kind of youthful fervor and dedication, and in many areas their activities and viewpoints overlap." In the same issue of the paper, the editor approved Goldwater's statement that the civil rights crisis would be solved only when men learned to love one another; legislation would be of no help. A noisy hassle broke out between Dr. McIntire and the Federal Communications Commission over the "Fairness Doctrine" concerning religious broadcasting (see p. 145). In several issues under full-page banner headlines, he charged the Democratic National Party, acting under political motivation, was attempting to deny him the use of the radio networks.[29]

The *Christian Beacon* faced a major editorial crisis when the question of Representative Miller's Roman Catholicism was raised. A reader asked if the editors "approved" of Goldwater's running mate. In the October 1 issue, on page 2, the managing editor replied.

> Who are we to "approve" of Goldwater? We agree with much of his program. He seems to be the only anti-Communist running. It behooves us to support him and pray for his election, but we have "approved" neither the man nor his running mate as individuals.

Then the editor stated the *Christian Beacon's* position on a Roman Catholic running on the national ticket. The statement was a complete reversal of the editorial policy taken when John F. Kennedy

---

tion. The only strongly conservative Protestant journal I know to criticize Goldwater's positions was *The Reformed Journal;* see XIV (July-Aug., 1964), pp. 3-4.

[29] *Christian Beacon,* July 23, 1964, pp. 6-7; see p. 1 of each issue of this journal from July 2 through September 17 for information on the dispute.

was a candidate in 1960. At that time the ACCC passed a resolution, printed by the *Christian Beacon*, stating that, "The Roman Church has already dedicated the United States to the Virgin Mary, and a Roman Catholic leader in the White House will advance that goal." In 1964 the same journal stated, on October 1,

> You ask our opinion of his running mate and again we can only say that we believe his record is more favorable to the influences for righteousness in our nation than the record of his opponent. The issue you are apparently trying to raise is hardly pertinent. Denominational lines don't determine degrees or limits of apostasy. Many Roman Catholics believe Christ was the virgin-born Son of God. Many who call themselves Protestants believe that He was not. Perhaps neither believe they are justified only through faith in Him, and therefore neither are saved, but of the two we have more respect for those who believe in the virgin birth than those who deny it.

There was no reference in 1964 to the Harlot of Babylon.

After the election, Dr. McIntire made public his support for Goldwater. In his judgment the individualistic ethic of fundamentalism was identical with the individualism of the Arizonian. "Protestants in the U. S. are for the most part conservatives, and don't forget that 27,000,000 of them voted for Goldwater." [30]

During the fall months Bundy avoided overt endorsement. The Church League publications carried articles which linked the New Frontier, the Great Society, and the Democratic administrations with the American Communist Party.[31] The league's major contribution was the title cited previously, "How the Communists and Religious Liberals Hate Barry Goldwater!" After the elections, the Wheaton office sent another letter, dated November 18.

---

[30] *Christian Beacon*, Aug. 19, 1965, p. 4; March 25, 1965, pp. 10-11; a Twentieth Century Reformation publication, "Christianity and Freedom" (1965); *Christian Beacon*, Jan. 21, 1965, p. 8, has another defense of Senator Goldwater.

[31] *News and Views*, July, 1964, entitled "Communist Advice for the 1964 Elections." Another 1964 *News and Views* was entitled "Arguments for Alger Hiss Apologist Used by Democratic National Committee to Pressure Anti-Communists Off Air"; this was a criticism of Fred Cook who had written the anti-Goldwater campaign book, *Barry Goldwater, Extremist of the Right,* and anti-radical right articles.

"There are at least 26 1/2 million Conservatives in the United States. Please, never lose sight of that fact." This was also the conclusion of virtually every ultrafundamentalist and far right spokesman during the postelection assessments. None denied that the Republicans had lost convincingly; all zealously asserted their fight for a conservative America had only begun.[32]

In summary, the fundamentalists of the far right had consciously and enthusiastically involved themselves for the first time in a national campaign; that was in itself a major reversal of their previous commitments. But more surprising was the zeal with which they were willing to cooperate with other far right groups which had shown no particular interest in what they as church members cherished most highly—total separation and pure doctrine. In other words, there were influences other than the zeal of the moment for a particular candidate which led the ultrafundamentalists to identify themselves with those citizens from whom they had stood aloof for so many years.

At least three historical and sociological factors helped lead these church people into a position where they could no longer be identified as "a peculiar people" (Titus 2:14). First, and most obvious, fundamentalists in and out of the ACCC–ICCC since World War II had voted the Republican ticket almost exclusively. Since it was the more conservative of the two national parties and since a citizen should always vote, the separationists voted Republican.[33]

Second, the ultrafundamentalists found the existence of an alliance between the political liberals of the Democratic Party and the theological liberals of the National Council of Churches. The record was clear. Both favored more civil rights for Negroes; both

---

[32] *New York Times,* Nov. 23, 1964, pp. 1, 42 by Donald Janson, who interviewed Walker, Smoot, Liberty officials, Hargis, Fulton Lewis III, Mrs. Phyllis Schlafly, and John Rousselot; see Lawrence Stern, "The Far Right Regroups," *The Progressive,* Feb., 1965, pp. 12-14.

[33] Among the empirical studies on this, see two articles by Benton Johnson, "Ascetic Protestantism and Political Preference," *Public Opinion Quarterly* XXVI (Spring, 1962), 35-46, and "Ascetic Protestantism and Political Preference in the Deep South," *American Journal of Sociology* LXIX (Jan., 1964), 359-66; see also Irving Crespi, "The Structural Basis for Right-Wing Conservatism: The Goldwater Case," Public Opinion Quarterly XXIX (Winter, 1965-66), 523-43; Ira S. Rohter, "The Radical Rightists: An Empirical Study," (Ph.D. diss., Michigan State University, 1967), chaps. 3-7.

violated the Constitution of the United States by interfering in the Southern states' rights to regulate voter registration. Both the liberals and the Democrats favored the president's war on poverty; both favored the Peace Corps; both were persistent critics of "Christian Conservatives." Had not Presidents Kennedy and Johnson openly cooperated with the National Council of Churches? Had not John F. Kennedy used the full power of his senatorial office in 1960 to discredit the Air Force Manual? Were not the presidential offices open to NCC leaders, but closed to those of the ACCC–ICCC? Had not the government ignored the ACCC protests over inviting Russian clergymen to visit America? The conclusion was inescapable; an organized conspiracy had been created to destroy the true Christians.

A third factor emerged as an issue helping to determine the direction of the ultrafundamentalists' politics. The Democrats since 1932 had received most of their support from urban centers, from minority and lower income groups, as well as from the great majority of intellectuals and labor unions and, to a lesser degree, from Roman Catholics. Few ultrafundamentalists were found in these groups. They identified the cities with extensive crime and violence, with pornography and sensuous dancing, with drinking and gambling, with lewd movies and dirty politics. The Democratic party was held accountable for introducing the many welfare laws and bureaucratic regulations which seemed un-American, confusing, and immoral.[34]

Within this milieu, as if a "blessing from God," the Republicans nominated a real conservative. Here was no me-too leap-year liberal, but an authentic, antibureaucratic, promorality, pro-simplicity candidate. And was it not possible that he shared the internal conspiracy thesis? During a speech in Maryland in mid-October, Goldwater said he would be willing to substitute another word for "soft" in the phrase "soft on Communism" to describe the Johnson foreign policy. From the audience "Voices cried 'Treason.' 'That's it' replied the Senator." [85]

[34] Richard Hofstadter, "Goldwater and His Party: The True Believer and the Radical Right," *Encounter* XXIII (Oct., 1964), 3-13; there is considerable empirical data in S. M. Lipset, "Beyond the Backlash," *Encounter* XXIII (Nov., 1964), 16-24; Richard Hofstadter, *Anti-Intellectualism in American Life* (New York: Alfred A. Knopf, 1963), pp. 131-36.
[85] *New York Times,* Oct. 21, 1964, p. 1; Oct. 28, 1964, p. 44.

As he traced the many problems of the day to the bungling of the national government, Senator Goldwater called for a rededication to individual integrity and personal responsibility to destroy the welfare state and growing bureaucracy. As did the ultrafundamentalists, he viewed socio-economic problems primarily as matters of individual responsibility rather than as products of discrimination, poverty, or congestion. The real problem in life was the power of sin, and that was a very personal influence. Once men had learned to turn back its worst influences, they could cope with the ills of this world.

For these reasons, and for the many elusive influences which help any voter make his choice, the ultrafundamentalists joined with the radical right in a concerted effort for Senator Goldwater. That choice was the culmination of the series of events set in motion by the career and death of Senator Joseph R. McCarthy and nurtured by the criticism of the New Frontier and the Great Society. To be sure, during the heated months following the assassination, the ACCC–ICCC leaders spoke in guarded terms on political issues. But their new outlook and the new enthusiasm for the cause was unmistakable.

In summarizing the major trends of fundamentalism of the far right since 1960, one notices, first, its rapid increase in financial strength and as a shaper of opinion and, second, the distinct submersion of its unique identity. The two trends were hardly unrelated. So long as the ACCC–ICCC had limited its focus to the realm of ecclesiastical and doctrinal controversy, it had attracted only miniscule support from the general public. But as the *Christian Beacon* itself noted, "Since 1960 sweeping changes in the growth and outreach of the Twentieth Century Reformation movement, paralleling in many ways the changes and development of the worldwide political conservative movement, have unfolded." [36] Its leaders learned how to improve their use of the mass media to promote their programs. This attracted enough revenue to purchase more radio time which, in turn, brought in more contributions.

[36] *Christian Beacon,* June 23, 1966, p. 3; this statement is especially revealing because it indicates that the ultrafundamentalists as well as their critics realized their movement did undergo a major change after John F. Kennedy became president.

Some of this fresh money came obviously from members of the American and International Councils. But a substantial, although immeasurable, portion came from church people outside these councils, who were not satisfied with the brand of anticommunism their own ministers were preaching. They wanted to hear church spokesmen expose the internal conspiracy, condemn the three steps to disaster, proclaim America a Christian nation, and demand total victory. If the ultrafundamentalist leaders were the only ministers saying these things, then they would be the men to support.

As the new alignment became evident, the issue of total separation was given only secondary priority among the major ultrafundamentalist spokesmen. The battle for God and against communism in all its forms overrode all other issues. The ACCC–ICCC welcomed nonseparationist contributions. Those donors chose to overlook the many criticisms heaped upon their own denominations by those to whom they contributed—that question seemed as far away as J. Gresham Machen. Now the prime question was: How did one stand on the internal conspiracy? That became the procrustean bed on which all Americans were measured by far rightists and ultrafundamentalists.[87]

This larger vision and greater involvement in world affairs gave to the ultrafundamentalist crusade a sense of purpose and direction it had not known in its early years of poverty and ridicule. That transformation, however, had exacted the price of identity. No longer were its members totally separate within Protestantism. Now the leaders were considered the leading church-related spokesmen for the entire far right cause. The two movements had become so inextricably intertwined in the first ten months of 1964 that no longer did they show the firm cleavage which had once been the cherished possession of the separationists.

The evidence for this conclusion can be found in pointing to the questions the ACCC–ICCC leaders have not answered. Their basic problem within Protestantism is to avoid cooperation with

[87] This conclusion is based largely on the material in the letters sent me when I asked in an article why so many nonseparationists supported McIntire, et al. See my "A New Protestant Realignment?" Concern, Nov. 1, 1965, pp. 10-14. This article was reprinted in the Christian Beacon and in McIntire's monthly fund-raising letter. Its appearance in these two places produced the mail to me.

any group or individual suspected of apostasy. So long as they limited themselves to ecclesiastical matters, they were faced with few problems. But when the far right movement took form in the late 1950's, its principles of patriotism and conservatism proved too attractive for the ultrafundamentalists to resist. Feeling the impact of civil rights agitation, the Great Society, the Stormer book, and Goldwater-Miller, they began saying nice things about nonseparationists who shared their ideology. That step was an admission that a citizen could be a true patriot without being a member of an ACCC–ICCC congregation, or even an independent, fundamentalist church. That step also implied that even a non-Christian could be a true patriot, since it was acknowledged that some devout Jews were honest anti-Communists. The conclusion to be drawn from these admissions is that patriotism does not ultimately depend on one's commitment to pure, fundamentalist doctrine.

The transformation by the "peculiar people" may be understood in another light. The ultrafundamentalist knows his faith is the most important part of his life; he must keep it pure at all costs. Yet, one must suggest, it is possible such pure faith is in some manner sullied or compromised when the fundamentalists of the far right work alongside and cooperate with patriots who themselves reject pure doctrine. The unanswered question here is: How can an ultrafundamentalist be sure that those outside his camp with whom he cooperates are free from apostasy? Since such a person has not renounced his membership in, say, an NCC and NAE denomination, then he has not had the courage to come out and be separate. *That* step is the ultimate test of one's loyalty to Christ, and that is the only test that matters.

Thus, the ultrafundamentalist is left cooperating with potential or real apostates in patriotic activities, but he separates himself from the most orthodox of nonseparated Christians who might not share his enthusiasm for far right action programs. Robert Welch, who has in print ridiculed fundamentalism and espouses an evolutionary humanism, receives praise from Drs. Hargis and McIntire, while in turn the *Christian Beacon* states that Carl F. H. Henry has shown a "soft hand" on communism and Billy Graham is condemned with equal zeal.

While these questions remain unanswered, there is no question over the fact that by the end of 1964, the fundamentalists of the far right were able to influence a portion of American Protestant thought beyond their membership. These five chapters have attempted to explain the historical forces which made possible the achievement of that power. The next chapter explores the formal biblical and theological foundations which undergird their politics of doomsday.

6
The Doctrines of Ultrafundamentalism

This chapter attempts to organize and examine the theology and ideology of fundamentalism of the far right. The four spokesmen make no pretense at offering a systematic outline of their doctrines. They are leaders of action programs rather than full time scholars, and have made no single, complete statement of their beliefs. Beyond that, they are not in total agreement on every issue. However their thought does reflect a substantial consensus which this chapter seeks to define.

The fundamentalist of the far right constructs his fortress for preserving Christianity and America on the rockbed of theological doctrine. Formal, precisely worded statements or "propositions" given to him by God in the Bible are the indestructible boulders of truth which eternally withstand the erosion of doubt, compromise, and ambiguity. They were created by God and are perfect and complete in themselves. So long as the believer accepts them as the Creator intended, he will be protected against the powers of evil and will preserve the true faith for all generations.

The entire theology and ideology of the ultrafundamentalist movement is based on its confidence in the efficacy of propositional doctrine. God has endowed the believer with sufficient reasoning powers to allow him to construct infallible statements. The statements are without error so long as they are based exclusively on the revealed word of God found in the inerrant Bible. The believer expresses his gratitude for such knowledge and witnesses to his faith by assenting to these doctrines. Men cannot know this truth unless it is expressed in a public manner open to scrutiny by other believers. Only propositional doctrine gives them that opportunity, thus only that form of expression is verifiable.[1]

Among the several creeds of Protestantism, the ultrafundamentalists give their highest allegiance to the statement of the American and International Councils of Christian Churches. This creed is carefully worded, both to establish pure doctrine and to avoid a precise definition of the controversial issues, such as the sacraments and the nature of the church, on which the ultrafundamentalists cannot agree among themselves. Disagreement on these matters but not on the "fundamentals" is permissible.

In several areas of doctrine, the teachings of the ACCC–ICCC harmonize with those of other conservative, orthodox Protestants, as for instance, the Trinity, the Virgin Birth, substitutionary atonement, physical resurrection, and conversion by the Holy Spirit. What follows in this chapter is an attempt to show (1) how the ultrafundamentalists' loyalty to their three most cherished doctrines—verbal inspiration and inerrancy of the Bible, total separation, and premillennial apocalypticism—preserves their distinctive position within fundamentalist circles, and (2) how they build the "politics of doomsday" on these foundations. For that reason, little attention is shown the other teachings mentioned just above although they are among the most treasured by all conservatives.

Since the Bible is the source of all knowledge, it must have

[1] William LeRoy, "A Christian Epistemology," *The Reformation Review* VIII (Jan., 1960), 107-8; the position on creeds is made clear in *Christian Beacon*, Jan. 26, 1967, pp. 4-5.

been inspired only by God. The ACCC–ICCC proof text (King James Version) is 2 Tim. 3:15-17. This is interpreted to mean:

> We believe in the divine inspiration and authority of the Scriptures. By this is meant a miraculous guidance of the Holy Spirit in their original writing, extending to all parts of the Scriptures equally, applying even to the choice of words, so that the result is the very Word of God, the only infallible rule of faith and practice. Moreover, it is our conviction that God has exercised such singular care and providence through the ages in preserving the written Word, that the Scriptures as we now have them are in every essential particular as originally given and contain all things necessary to salvation.[2]

This viewpoint is known as "verbal inspiration," almost identical with that of the Hodge-Warfield "Princeton Theology" of the nineteenth century. To it are often added the words "full" or "plenary" to reinforce the point that each word in all sixty-six books is equally inspired.

What makes the ultrafundamentalists' understanding unique among conservatives is their willingness to believe in the "dictation method" of inspiration. The ACCC–ICCC teachings on this issue, to be sure, flatly reject the charge made by some critics that they are saying each biblical writer acted as a robot or stenographer copying down by dictation exactly what he was told, word by word, without contributing any of his own literary style. However, a careful look at ultrafundamentalist leaders' statements indicates they do accept the dictation position. Dr. McIntire wrote, "The Bible is the Word of God because its inspiration extended even to the precise word used and chosen to convey God's message to man." An editorial in the *Christian Beacon* explains that the mind of God is found in the Bible, "authenticated by each writer as he took it down as being inspired by God the Holy Spirit." [3]

[2] Shelton College *Bulletin, 1965-1966,* p. 14; this is a college of the ACCC; *Christian Beacon*, Sept. 15, 1966, pp. 2-3; other proof texts are listed in Carl McIntire, *The Death of a Church,* chap. 2.

[3] LeRoy, "A Christian Epistemology," p. 111; *Christian Beacon,* March 26, 1964, p. 2; March 16, 1961, p. 6; Aug. 5, 1965, pp. 2-3; and Sept. 10, 1959, p. 4; McIntire, *Death of a Church,* pp. 20-21; see McIntire's pamphlet, "Twelve Reasons Why the Bible Is the Word of God," p. 4; *Christian Beacon,* Aug. 19,

Recognizing that the translations today were not themselves directly inspired, and accepting the explanation that only the first editions ("autographa") were inerrant, the ACCC–ICCC members nonetheless hold unswervingly to the idea they can make no mistakes in discerning God's truth. Dr. Hargis states, "I do not believe there is a single error in the text of the King James Bible." An ACCC official spelled it out, "I claim, therefore, that we, as Bible-believing Christians and as a council of Christian churches, have all the answers and are well able to answer every man." [4] Nothing, absolutely nothing, which fails to harmonize with his understanding is true; it is as simple as that.

In brief summary, the ultrafundamentalist deduces that the Bible is either completely false or completely 'inerrant' by his definition. Those who disagree are guilty not only of academic error but of

the murder of children! People who reject the final authority of the Scriptures, renounce the fundamentals of historic Christianity and fail to rescue precious souls from sin through the preaching of justification by faith are guilty of murder.[5]

Since nonbelievers will live for eternity in a hell of real fire and torture, they practice murder by failing to instruct their children in the fundamentals of the faith.

Lest anyone think the ultrafundamentalist is claiming for himself perfect knowledge based on his own resources, the spokesmen point out their judgments are freed from error because of two things God has made available: the substitutionary atonement of Christ, which removed from believers the corruption of original sin on one's judgment, and, second, the on-going, indwelling power of the Holy Spirit to keep the believer pure until the Final Judgment. As was seen in the exchange of letters with

1965, p. 2; Sept. 10, 1964, p. 8; and a brief summary in Sept. 15, 1966, issue, pp. 2-3.
    [4] Hargis in a Christian Crusade pamphlet, "What's Wrong With Jesus"; The Rev. Ralph Yarnell, *Christian Beacon*, May 29, 1958, p. 3; March 26, 1964, p. 2; April 2, 1964, p. 2; "Guiding Principles in a Day of Apostasy," ACCC Literature Item no. 103, pp. 6, 8.
    [5] *Christian Beacon*, July 23, 1964, pp. 2, 6; May 8, 1958, pp. 1, 2, 4, 8; Nov. 4, 1948, p. 5.

Dr. E. Stanley Jones (pp. 53-54), the ACCC–ICCC member feels freed from the judgment of God and thus ignores any criticism of his theology, his politics, his science or anything else outside his tradition because he cannot err.

The second distinctive doctrine of ultrafundamentalism, total separation, has its sources in the view of the Bible just discussed. Those not accepting God's eternal truth cannot help but err in judging the Scriptures; therefore, to follow their teachings would be to destroy the Christian faith itself. To protect the eternal truths until the bodily return of Jesus for the millennium, the born-again believer must carry out his mission by having nothing whatsoever to do with those who destroy God's word by failing to agree with him.

Once separated, he learns the outside world misunderstands his motives, especially his frequent and often acrimonious criticisms of those outside the fold. "Separation involves controversy—hard, gruelling controversy. It involves attacks—personal attacks, even violent attacks. It involves salaries—food, houses, it tests faith." Such a stand is, to McIntire, "an expression of Christian love. An aggressive stand against the forces of unbelief is the highest and deepest expression of love for Christ." [6] This does not mean, as critics have charged, that the believer lacks kindness or forbearance. McIntire writes, "Satan preaches brotherly love in order to hold men in the apostasy." No ACCC–ICCC member has any dealing with any ministerial council or interdenominational activities. One ACCC clergyman instructed his flock not to invite any "apostate minister" to their Sunday dinner.[7]

Knowing he alone, to sum up, understands God's Word and keeps himself pure by total separation, the ultrafundamentalist chooses "apocalyptic premillennialism" as his interpretation of what will happen in the Last Days. The ACCC–ICCC creed proclaims "His resurrection from the dead in the same body in which He was crucified, and the second coming of this same Jesus in power and great glory. The everlasting bliss of the saved, and the everlasting suffering of the lost."

[6] Carl McIntire, "Testimony of Separation" (Collingswood, N. J.: Christian Beacon Press, 1952), p. 44; Christian Beacon, Feb. 24, 1955, p. 4.
[7] McIntire, "Testimony of Separation," pp. 79, 97; Christian Beacon, Aug. 27, 1964, p. 2.

This means: We believe in the visible, personal and premillennial return of our Lord Jesus Christ for His Church, and the establishment of a worldwide kingdom of righteousness and peace with His redeemed.[8]

While the fundamentalists of the far right allow for some differences of opinion on certain details concerning the last things, they stand united on the major teachings as they interpret them from the Book of Revelation and the prophecies of Matthew 24-26.

Every ultrafundamentalist believes the prophecies are being fulfilled—the last days are here, right now. This conviction dominates their thought so thoroughly as to color every pronouncement they make on theological and political issues. Everywhere around them they find the world crumbling, old standards being swept away, loyalty to pure doctrine being destroyed, and the work of Satan reigning throughout Christendom.

Apostasy of apostasies, says the ultrafundamentalist, all is apostasy. Those posing as Christians are rapidly destroying the faith of our fathers. They can be found in high places and in low; they can be found in colleges, seminars, local congregations, and denominational headquarters, in Protestant, Catholic, and Jewish groups, among the rich and the poor, the highly educated and the average man. All this points to "that great hour when the Son of God shall appear and when indeed there shall be a mighty meeting in the sky."[9]

Quite literally, Satan is ready to reappear on this earth. He is clever enough not to appear as the representative of evil, but he will pose as a great religious savior, who is really the Antichrist. The true Christian will not despair over the coming of

[8] Shelton College Catalog, 1965-1966, p. 14; Faith Theological Seminary Catalog, 1963-1965, p. 35 states it teaches premillennialism but says nothing about dispensationalism; Bundy's views on eschatology are in News and Views, Dec., 1964; for the relationship of the ACCC to dispensationalism see C. C. Ryrie, Dispensationalism Today (Chicago: Moody Press, 1964), pp. 80-81, 100, 106.
[9] Christian Beacon, March 4, 1965, pp. 4-5; Oct. 7, 1965, pp. 2-3; McIntire's packet, "The Meeting in the Skies," p. 1, reprinted in the Christian Beacon, Feb. 24 and March 3, 1966; see Hargis' views in Christian Crusade, March, 1966, pp. 11-12 and May, 1965, p. 12; a pamphlet by Allan A. MacRae, "The Premillennial Return of Christ," published by Faith Theological Seminary.

131

Satan. He will be spared any suffering because just before Satan achieves his victory, the believer will experience the "pretribulation rapture." The righteous dead will be brought to life and together with the saving remnant still alive on earth will be physically raised up and lifted (raptured) into the skies. There they will live with Jesus and be reunited with their loved ones. They will live in the skies for seven years.[10]

Just after the Rapture, God will allow the Great Tribulation to sweep over the earth. This is a period of seven years of unrelieved physical and mental horror when the Devil, the Antichrist, takes command of this world. It will mean:

> Satanic delusion, demonism, and Antichrist enslavement (Rev. 13:16-18) will sweep the earth, producing fearful suffering, martyrdom, and death. Under the seven-headed Beast (Antichrist) centralized power will develop and lead to destructive judgment of religious (Rev. 17) and civil Babylon (Rev. 18). Supernatural warfare will cause indescribable conditions. All will climax in the trinity of hell (Rev. 13) as it endeavors to displace the Trinity of the Godhead.[11]

McIntire warns his audience, "The atom bomb is a fearful thing, but this Tribulation, which is described by the prophets, this Day of Wrath, the Day of the Lord, and what it is going to mean, and what it is going to do on earth is infinitely more dreadful. You had better think about fleeing and get ready to escape in those days, as our Saviour said. Accept Christ as your Saviour and then you will be caught up with the Church when the time comes for us to go, and it can be any moment."[12]

Then comes the fulfillment so deeply awaited by all Christians—the Battle of Armageddon. This will be the final cataclysmic conflict between good and evil. On the one hand will stand the Antichrist and his armies, fully armed, dedicated, without

[10] McIntire, "The Meeting in the Skies," p. 2; *Christian Beacon,* March 4, 1965, p. 3, shows some ultrafundamentalists hold to a posttribulation position.
[11] *Christian Beacon,* Oct. 7, 1965, p. 2; Hargis, *Christian Crusade,* March, 1966, pp. 12-13. The organization linking Hargis to the ICCC, the International Conference of Calvary Tabernacles, concentrates heavily on eschatological prophecy in its broadcasts and publications.
[12] "The Battle of Armageddon," *Christian Beacon,* Sept. 21, 1967, p. 8.

scruple. On the other will stand Christ and his army from heaven. Ultrafundamentalists agree the battle will be fought at Megiddo, "right there near Jerusalem, just a little northeast of the city. Here is Jerusalem. Here is the Mount of Olives, and here comes our Saviour to bring a final great consummation to the great promises He made to Abraham, to Isaac, and to Jacob." The results will be the most important event since Pentecost; "The Gentile world system will come to an end at the Battle of Armageddon." [13]

McIntire explains further. "Thank God, I will get a view of the Battle of Armageddon from the grandstand seats of the heavens. All who are born again will see the Battle of Armageddon, but it will be from the skies." Then Jesus, with those he raptured, will return to earth to usher in the millennium. He will place his feet first on the Mount of Olives to fulfill prophecy (Zech. 14:4). At that point he will be joined by "the redeemed of every age, the hosts of heaven, and all the angels of heaven."

For a thousand years they will live on earth.

The Scriptures declare that a reign of universal blessedness, including freedom from both war and fear of war, is to be set upon the earth. However, God the Son will Himself establish this in the time of God's sovereign choosing, without human aid, and then even the wild beasts and tame animals will lie down at peace with one another.[14]

Satan will have one more opportunity to regain the earth. Following the thousand years he will be released from prison and attempt once more to lead men to reject Christ and accept him. This will be a brief but violent age, climaxed by the physical destruction of the forces of evil with fire from heaven.

Doomsday then comes to this planet. Christ will come again on a cloud and take his seat on the great white throne. This world and this universe as man knows it will be destroyed. Every wicked person will be brought back to life in the same body in which he lived. One by one, each will come before Christ the Judge, and

[13] Ibid.; Christian Crusade, March, 1966, p. 13.
[14] Christian Beacon, June 24, 1965, p. 5; McIntire, "The Meeting in the Skies," pp. 1-2; McIntire's pamphlet "Why Christians Believe in the Second Coming of Christ," passim.

will hear an angel read the list of his every deed and thought as written in the book of life. Jesus will cast all of them into the actual hell of fire and punishment. Then he will turn the saved into "the most beautiful individuals that we could possibly imagine and it will be His handiwork and by the grace of God." [15]

The true Christian will live with his glorified body eternally with the Godhead, the fulfillment of God's plans which he had made before creating this world. The believer cannot say more about heaven because God has chosen to reveal that knowledge only when he has his children with him. One thing is known.

> Is it not marvelous that when we all get to Heaven there will not be any Modernists? No, they are not going to make it. Is it not marvelous that, when we get to Heaven and the new heavens and the new earth have shown their glory, and we turn back and read these passages in Isaiah about the new heavens and the new earth, we will all be fundamentalists? [16]

The ultrafundamentalist's loyalty to apocalyptic premillennialism leads him to take direct action. He defends the local, independent church because he believes any trend toward centralization points to the "coming one-world church." He repudiates the United Nations and the World Council of Churches and the increasing rule of world law for the same reason.

> In the Book of Revelation, the scarlet woman, representing the ecclesiastical world power, rides upon the back of the beast, representing the one-world political power. Here we see the ecclesiastical power of the World Council of Churches counselling and seeking to direct the affairs of the governments of the world as they deal with communism, and this pressure is on the side of surrender to communism in the Far East.[17]

These doctrines also directly shape the ultrafundamentalist attitude toward the cold war. America need not fear communism

[15] *Christian Beacon,* March 25, 1965, p. 7; McIntire, *Author of Liberty,* p. 228; McIntire, "The Meeting in the Skies," pp. 1-2.

[16] McIntire, "The Meeting in the Skies," p. 2.

[17] *Christian Beacon,* May 12, 1955, p. 8; Hargis, *Christian Crusade,* May, 1965, p. 12.

in its Soviet or Chinese forms, even though these nations have nuclear weapons. America allowed the Reds to expand and dominate much of the world out of fear that its resistance might precipitate the destruction of life on this planet. However, prophecy clearly shows this world will be destroyed *only* by the direct act of God during the last judgment; neither nuclear weapons nor any other man-made instruments will accomplish that. Hence, America must use its full military might to resist Communist expansion and to overthrow its governments around the globe. The Communists will not retaliate with destructive weapons. Only God can destroy what he gave man.[18]

On the domestic scene, since it is inevitable that evil will eventually dominate the affairs of men, the only recourse for the believer is to prepare for the Final Judgment. By becoming involved in reform programs of an economic or social nature, a citizen misplaces his energy and time. This world as it stands is hopelessly evil. Thus the Christian must cleanse himself now because the last days are here.

However, God in his wisdom has provided sufficient grace for those who believe his promises. He has shown man what he expects of him and has given man the opportunity to express his gratitude. Man praises God by formal worship, by loyalty to pure doctrine and by devoted participation in the society which most accurately reflects God's will for man, the United States of America.

The Twentieth Century Reformation Hour proclaims it is "putting more Christianity in the Patriots, and More Patriotism in the Christians." As its guiding principle, Christian Crusade states it "is unswervingly committed to the cause of New Testament Christianity—and militantly stands against its enemies. As champions of Christian Americanism, we are equally determined." The Church League of America states as its first principle "We must rekindle the spirit of Christian Americanism." The founder of the American Council of Christian Laymen wrote, "Christianity, free, representative government, and free enterprise working together, in harmony for better things—that is America."

[18] As expressed by Dr. McIntire on a radio broadcast, KUXL, Minneapolis, June 14, 1966.

135

The ultrafundamentalists identify themselves with the full far right movement in their mutual promotion of Christian Americanism. While their exclusivist theology has little broad appeal, their religious nationalism has endeared them to every faction of the radical right. Together the two wings celebrate the principles of republican self-government and laissez-faire free enterprise as their answer to the powers of the internal conspiracy. These teachings are as inerrant as the Bible, which is the source of their inspiration and authority.

The ultrafundamentalist finds republican self-government clearly endorsed in Scripture. Conceding that no specific prophecy as such foretells the founding of Christian America, Dr. Hargis explains:

Christian educators have long realized that our concept of freedom and government is established upon the Bible teaching that man is made in the image of God, possessed of God-given rights, and invested with responsibilities and duties to his Creator and his fellowman. Our cherished rules of honor, integrity, and morality, which are the criterion of good citizenship in this nation are lifted from the pages of this Holy Book.[19]

Nowhere was God's concern for America made more clear than in the 1780's. "A Constitution was desired which would express, in terms of orderly government, the aspirations of the commoners." The nation's most prominent leaders met at Philadelphia and forged the greatest constitution in the history of civilization. Its basic principles rested on the scriptural doctrines of liberty, justice, and freedom. "What must be understood is that the document which is the supreme law of the land recognizes the presence and providence of God and that no law is just unless it is shown to be in accord with His special revelation found in the Bible." To this testimony by the Founding Fathers has been added over the years the witness of faith of great national leaders: Daniel Webster, Andrew Jackson, Abraham Lincoln, Woodrow

[19] "Threats to Christian Education," pp. 2-3; see also his pamphlet, "What's Wrong with Jesus?"; Bundy in News and Views, July, 1962, passim.

Wilson, and Calvin Coolidge, to name but a few. This is unimpeachable proof of America's Christian foundations.[20]

Long before the John Birch Society made it one of its slogans, the leaders of the ACCC–ICCC argued that the United States is a republic, not a democracy. They find a biblical basis for differentiation between the two forms of government. "Democracy" means government by the people and "republic" means government by law and more specifically, by God's law. While the former is subject to self-interest and emotion, the latter rests on universal, time-proven principles. The Founding Fathers chose that form of government.

This means "in administering the affairs of men, the State must be guided by the laws that God has made for man. Thus the State literally becomes a servant of God, and this is exactly what is taught in the Bible." To some observers this may sound close to "the divine right of kings" but to McIntire it means men are guaranteed freedom because God is the author of liberty. A Christian Crusader states that ultimate governmental sovereignty does not reside in the people but with the resurrected and ascended Lord Jesus Christ now in heaven, "where He reigns as sovereign Lord over all things, including the public affairs of these United States." Mr. Kaub devoted considerable attention to this theme. "Democracy is synonymous with socialism." It is anti-Christian because it claims that the voice of the people is the voice of God. The Founding Fathers rejected such views and established a republic based on God's eternal laws.[21]

The supreme joy for the ultrafundamentalist is his use of these teachings to draw up his indictment of liberalism. Be it political, theological, or economic, liberalism to him stands far

[20] *Christian Beacon*, March 13, 1958, p. 2; Kaub, *Collectivism*, pp. 13-16; McIntire, *Author of Liberty*, p. 109; Hargis, "America—Let's Get Back to God," pp. 5-10; *Christian Beacon*, Feb. 13, 1964, p. 3 and Sept. 23, 1965, p. 3. Obviously, many historians today would question how widespread the "commoner" demand was for a new constitution.

[21] McIntire, *Author of Liberty*, pp. 109-10; *Christian Beacon*, Jan. 12, 1967, p. 3; a sermon by the Rev. T. Robert Ingram in the Christian Crusade pamphlet, "Highlights; Christian Crusade Third Annual Anti-Communist Leadership School, 1964," pp. 11-14; Verne P. Kaub, *Communist-Socialist Propaganda in American Schools* (Madison: American Council of Christian Laymen, 1960), pp. 102-16.

above every "ism," every other system of ideas as the ultimate weapon used by Satan to destroy Christian America. To preserve the true faith the believer must draw on every resource at his disposal; nothing he does is more important than exposing and destroying "The Liberal Establishment."

It is at this precise point in the ideology of fundamentalism of the far right that the objectives of the movement are the most clearly understood. The leaders and supporters hate and fight communism with an indignation born of their religious convictions. In the name of anti-communism they conclude that liberalism is the inevitable first step to socialism; socialism is the inevitable twin sister of communism. Just as no gradations or nuances are possible in their propositional theological doctrine, so too they allow no shadings in their condemnation of every system of government and economic organization which fails to meet their standards. A citizen has two choices; fundamentalism of the far right or doing the work of Satan.

Dr. Hargis captures the essence of the politics of doomsday:

Of this I am certain: Whatever happens, as Christians and Conservatives, we are on the winning team. It is quite possible that the American people will rise and give the Liberals a political thrashing at the polls next year. If however, the Lord does not will a victory for the Christian Conservative minority, then we have the promise of the Second Coming of Christ, God will not sit by and see His church crucified on the Communist cross. One crucifixion in His lifetime was enough.

We will either win in 1968 and preserve Christian constitutional government, which include freedom of speech for the Conservative fundamental Christian minority, or the nation will continue to plunge headlong into captivity which will necessitate the Second Coming of Christ to take His church out of this unbelieving world, hellbent on its own destruction.[22]

[22] A Christian Crusade pamphlet, "The Death of Freedom of Speech in the U.S.A.," pp. 39-40; John H. Redekop, *The American Far Right: A Case Study of Billy James Hargis and Christian Crusade* (Grand Rapids: Eerdmans Publishing Co., 1968), pp. 45, 59, 81, 98, 103.

The objections to liberalism, which is really communism in disguise, rest on ultrafundamentalist doctrine. Hargis finds it to be "veiled or concealed atheism." "Communism, at least, is open atheism; but Liberalism is concealed atheism." Since the Bible teaches only two answers to every question, and since conservatism obviously harmonizes with the Bible, it must follow that any variation, however slight, must harmonize with atheism.

The fundamentalists of the far right take this conclusion into areas of political thought others have never explored. They point out that liberalism leads America not only into communism, but also into nazism at the same time. One Christian Crusader explains: "After the Liberal has the people thoroughly his—and they are always his as they smack their oily and greedy lips and enjoy advantages they have not earned by hard work—then the Liberal really moves in on them, with the knout and the whip, with the sword and fire and the club, finally with guns and concentration camps and massacres." [23]

Hargis explains, "I consider fascism a part of Marxism or communism, and I am totally opposed to Marxism, communism, socialism, and liberalism." "Socialism inheres in the Nazi ideology as it does in communism and in liberalism. American Liberals and American Nazis derive from Karl Marx, his welfare state and socialism." [24]

This conviction leads Hargis to claim that the late George Lincoln Rockwell, leader of the American Nazi Party, was a front or stooge for the liberals and the Anti-Defamation League. His argument points out that by having Rockwell condemn the left-wing in racist, hate-filled terms, the liberals would insure that the public lumped together all right-wing groups, such as Christian Crusade, with the Nazis. They would, in Hargis' judgment, associate Christian Conservatives with Nazis. Admitting he has no documentation to prove this, he charged that the Anti-Defamation League "traffics in fear—fear in the hearts of the Jews—in order to stimulate funds." Apparently the research department

[23] Taylor Caldwell, "The Yellow Travelers," *Christian Crusade,* Oct. 1966, p. 9.
[24] Redekop, *The American Far Right,* pp. 83-84; a letter to the editor by Billy James Hargis in *The Covenant Companion* (Evangelical Covenant Church of America), Jan. 12, 1968, p. 2.

of Christian Crusade, of which Hargis boasts so frequently, had not been able to furnish him with evidence for that charge. No responsible scholars, to this author's knowledge, have seriously considered the allegation that the Jewish people support Nazis. Neither McIntire, Bundy, nor even Kaub with his anti-Semitism, expressed any agreement with Hargis' linkage of liberals, Nazis, and the Anti-Defamation League.[25]

The second major doctrine of this form of religious nationalism is laissez-faire free enterprise, which to Dr. McIntire is "the very foundation structure of society itself in which men are to live and render an account of themselves to God." His prime proof text is the Eighth Commandment, "Thou Shalt Not Steal." God has given man an absolute right to hold property; no man nor government can deny him that right. "It is his to do with as he pleases." [26] Such property must be obtained for the purpose of providing food and shelter for the capitalist and his family. In this process he learns that competition for property cannot be avoided. This, too, is part of God's plan. Competition helps reinforce the concept of stewardship. The owner has the responsibility to obtain as much additional property as he can. As a steward of God's gifts, he must turn two talents into four, five talents into ten. Competition will help guide him to use his property wisely and industriously.

The Christian property owner knows God wants him to enjoy his property; the profit motive and acquisition are not the products of his sin or greed. On the contrary, a well-to-do capitalist knows God is blessing him; his success shows the world he is a man of self-discipline and high character. He understands his responsibility for setting a good example. He avoids dissipation, he shuns laziness, he enjoys hard work. He realizes above all these are gifts from God and he must use them for the glory of his Creator.

Since the Ten Commandments in no manner deal with the civil government, it is obvious that the government has no mandate

[25] *Christian Crusade,* July, 1967, pp. 11-13.
[26] Although they often use the terms "free enterprise" and "capitalism" interchangeably, the ultrafundamentalists prefer "free" or "private enterprise." See Allan A. MacRae, "Communism and the Historic Christian Faith," pp. 10-12, and two McIntire pamphlets, "Private Enterprise in the Scriptures" and "Why I Am a Capitalist."

from God to tell the capitalist how he must use his property. So long as the civil government limits itself to protecting the right of the individual to compete for property, it acts in accord with God's commands. At those times when capitalists act unlawfully, the government must step in as a policeman to protect the honest citizen.

This theme has been thoroughly explored in a pamphlet first published by Mr. Kaub and now sold by the Laymen's Commission of the ACCC—Ray Carroll's "Jesus, A Capitalist." When living in Nazareth, Jesus was a capitalist. He worked with Joseph as a building contractor. They had no labor union to disrupt their business; prices were fixed by haggling. The two carpenters participated in competitive bidding. They bought materials from the caravans passing through. They learned to be shrewd dealers in the face of heavy competition. From these experiences Jesus learned much about human nature, especially when it would be wise to allow short-term credit. He "would know that he must keep a sharp eye out on payday, otherwise old Zebedee never would get beyond the tavern with a farthing. Booze was booze in Nazareth then, just as it is in Washington city today." "Jesus was a capitalist, preaching a doctrine of individualism which is the basis of free enterprise, and for this the religious and political hierarchies contrived his death."

All ultrafundamentalists point to Ephesians 4:28 as their prime proof text for free enterprise. "Let him that stole steal no more; but rather let him labour, working with his hands the thing which is good, that he may have to give to him that needeth." Private property is exonerated, private benevolence is endorsed. One finds no mention of government involvement.

God has always continued to approve the private ownership of property. The history of Western civilization since Pentecost proves that in those societies where the Bible was correctly interpreted, the citizenry had practiced laissez-faire free enterprise. This was fully apparent in the economy of Geneva led by John Calvin. The hard-working Protestants then believed that holiness consisted not only of personal piety, but of developing the virtues of industry, thrift, prudence, and self-discipline. God expected them to make a profit; that could be done honestly only by living

141

up to the terms of biblical capitalism. The authors of the early Protestant creeds also understood this principle and wrote it into their formal confessions.[27]

The final set of facts to prove God favored this form of free enterprise is found in the pages of American history. God endowed this nation with every possible blessing: rich soil, moderate climate, ample minerals, and an inventive people. In its early years, the United States followed his will by organizing its economy along biblical guidelines. By the twentieth century it had become the most wealthy and powerful nation in world history. Nothing less than the approval of God could explain that phenomenon.[28]

Just as the principles of historic, republican self-government have immediate relevance for today's liberal-conservative conflict, so too the principles of biblical capitalism must be restored to their original purity. The ACCC–ICCC spokesmen believe God has called them to that task. They see, as Kaub has diagrammed, three interlocking circles—Christianity, free government, and free enterprise. While Christianity could survive without the latter two, Americans could never recapture their original purity by ignoring those two principles.

These circles not only embrace certain values; they also exclude unwanted increments. They keep out any moderation, any compromise, or any change from the standards they believe were set by the Founding Fathers. The three circles exclude the "welfare state," "human rights over property rights," "deficit financing," or "the war on poverty." Such practices or values are not only wrong in economic thinking; they are sins against the Bible.

This form of religious nationalism emerges logically from the ultrafundamentalist mode of reasoning. The doctrine of verbal inspiration establishes the existence of absolute, indivisible truth which is factually verifiable. One cannot understand this truth unless he believes that its expression in the inerrant Bible stands triumphantly above all man-made efforts to destroy it. That source alone furnishes its believers with precise answers to every question

[27] MacRae, "Communism and the Historic Christian Faith," *passim;* a pamphlet widely circulated in far right circles, Edward Greenfield, "A Clergyman Reconsiders Free Enterprise"; McIntire, *Tyrant,* chap. 10.

[28] Hargis, "America—Let's Get Back to God," p. 9; McIntire, *Author of Liberty,* pp. 118-19.

142

in life. To protect this truth for all generations, the true Christian separates from the first signs of apostasy. The corrupted world in its anger will reject the believer's faith and will seek to destroy him. He must resist with every resource God has given him. When he seems to be losing, he knows he is winning because God is bringing this world to its final destruction. Thus, even as self-government and free enterprise seemed doomed to destruction, the ultrafundamentalist rejoices. The first skirmishes before the pretribulation rapture are now being fought; the Final Judgment is not far off. The reward is citizenship in the Heavenly City populated only by fundamentalists.

7
An Alliance for Action

The fundamentalist of the far right knows his fortress of pure doctrine can withstand any weapon Satan hurls against it. He also knows he cannot simply remain within its walls, enjoying its safety and security. God has appointed him to march out into the world to contend earnestly for the faith. This chapter seeks to explain how the ultrafundamentalist uses his doctrines in action programs to identify the enemy and to preserve Christian America.

The starting point for action is the call to arms. America must be alerted before Satan carries off the victory. No one needs to be a scholar, an expert, a "Harvard radical" to know what the Devil is doing. Most Americans know Russian and Chinese communism is evil. What most of them do not know, however, is how brilliantly the Devil has introduced communism into the mainstream of American life. The call to arms must thus be sounded against the enemy at home. Former Major General Edwin A. Walker gave the command to the entire far right when he stated, "no man can be a Communist, a Socialist, or a Kennedy liberal and follow the teachings of Christ." [1]

The proof of the Kennedy attempt to brainwash America is found in the enforcement of the "Fairness Doctrine" of the Federal Communications Commission. In 1948, the commission announced it would require radio stations to extend without charge the opportunity for anyone criticized to reply on the same station. At that time little controversy developed, primarily because so few broadcasts were being made by the far right. Not until 1960, with the emergence of the candidacy of Senator Kennedy, did the FCC find the need for applying its earlier ruling. As the number of radical right programs increased, especially those critical of Catholicism and the New Frontier desegregation policies, the FCC was asked by two perennial targets of such criticism, Walter and Victor Reuther, to clarify and enforce the 1949 policy. The brothers sent Attorney General Robert F. Kennedy a memorandum suggesting how the FCC might implement its doctrine in light of the rapidly changing political climate. Their statement became known as the "Reuther Memorandum," dated December, 1961, and widely circulated by far right groups. The latter, including the ACCC–ICCC leaders, became convinced this memo served as the basis for a revised policy announced by the commission in July, 1963.[2]

The key provision read:

In determining compliance with the fairness doctrine the Commission looks to substance rather than to label for form. It is immaterial whether a particular program or viewpoint is presented under the label of "Americanism," "anticommunism" or "state's rights," or whether it is a paid announcement, official speech, editorial, or religious broadcast. Regardless of label or form, if one viewpoint of a controversial

[1] As quoted in Barnet Baskerville, "The Cross and the Flag: Evangelists of the Far Right," *The Official Journal of the Western Speech Association* XXVII (Fall, 1963), 201.

[2] The full text of the Doctrine is in FCC, "Public Notice 'B' " July 26, 1963; see a Christian Crusade pamphlet, "The Fairness Doctrine—What's Fair About It?," and the Hargis pamphlet, "Walter Reuther's Secret Memorandum"; also the Manion Forum pamphlet, "The Reuther Memorandum" (South Bend, Indiana), and "Dan Smoot Report" (Dallas, Texas) for June 29, 1964 and Sept. 16, 1963.

issue of public importance is presented, the licensee is obligated to make a reasonable effort to present the other opposing viewpoint or viewpoints.

In the judgment of the far right the federal government had singled out its programs for special regulation. The FCC statement mentioned only "Americanism," or "anti-Communist" or "state's rights" programs. If the doctrine were to pertain to the left wing, then its wording should have been made explicit. The omission could only mean, in far right understanding, that the Kennedy-Reuther Establishment had struck down freedom of speech.

The spokesmen for the ACCC–ICCC soon learned, however, that conservative opinion across the nation was not unanimously hostile to the updated policy. An editorial writer for the Southern Baptist Journal, *Baptist Program,* suggested the FCC could now prevent personal attacks by those who "have impugned the patriotism, intelligence, motives, and loyalty to Christ of all those who differ from the extreme right-wing fundamentalist theological and political viewpoint of the speakers." [3] Without having to establish actual censorship, the FCC could insure that those attacked would have opportunity for rebuttal. The issue was taken to the Supreme Court, where in 1969, the justices upheld the doctrine by a 7 to 0 vote.

The entire radical right is convinced that if it could bring its indictment of the internal conspiracy directly to the people, its membership ranks would swell into the millions. Much of its organized activity centers on presenting its set of facts to prove the great betrayal. The following section is a summary of how the ultrafundamentalists and the far right identify the enemy within.

Nowhere is the liberal-socialist-Communist stranglehold over America more complete than in the distorted picture the public has been given on foreign policy developments since World War II. In the judgment of the far right, America has failed completely to halt the advance of communism and, by no coincidence—"little or nothing is being done officially to stop it." [4]

[3] As cited in *Baptist Message,* May 21, 1964, p. 4; this is the official journal of the Louisiana Baptist Convention of the Southern Baptist Convention.
[4] Hargis, Newsletter, Feb. 14, 1961, p. 1.

They believe the American government deliberately aided Communists. The Department of State has been controlled since 1933 by known Red fronters, dupes, one-worlders, and bleeding hearts. Its policy makers would rather negotiate than risk conflict. What else could explain the existence of American trade with Red Poland and Red Yugoslavia; any help given to any Communist nation for any reason helps Satan. The United States, as a Christian nation, should have no relations with any atheistic country.[5]

In harmony with their doctrine of total separation, the ACCC–ICCCC leaders are convinced God has commanded them to abstain from any dealings with non-Christians. Only a pure witness can accomplish God's purposes on earth, and only the ultrafundamentalists maintain that purity. Those nations who disagree with American policy have the privilege of ignoring it.[6]

The world cannot survive half-enslaved; the sooner everyone knows that the sooner communism can be destroyed. The leading fundamentalists of the far right insist, however, that their policy will not lead to intercontinental nuclear war. They believe America should be more realistic about achieving peace on this planet. The ACCC made its position clear in 1959. It "is not so blind or naïve to believe in the possibility of peace as the world offers it." Believing the only peace is that "given by Christ to the blood-washed soul," the council states "there is no peace to the wicked, and that there will be wars and rumors of wars until the end of the age."[7]

Dr. McIntire wrote, in 1946, before the Soviets had exploded their first nuclear device:

America used the atomic bomb at Hiroshima as an instrument for freedom. It worked. For just the same reason America should now use the atomic power at the present moment,

[5] A Hargis pamphlet, "This I Believe," p. 5; *Christian Beacon*, May 7, 1959, p. 2; Hargis, *Communism—The Total Lie*, pp. 30-31; Carl McIntire, *The Death of a Church*, chap. 9; Redekop, *The American Far Right*, chap. 4.

[6] See McIntire's pamphlet, "Red China and her Slaves"; also ACCC Literature Item no. 300, "National Council of Churches and Red China"; McIntire's pamphlet, "Christian Repudiation of Coexistence"; Hargis, *Communism—The Total Lie*, chap. 8.

[7] *Christian Beacon*, Oct. 22, 1959, p. 3.

if necessary. If she does not, she is failing her stewardship before God.[8]

In another area of foreign policy, the ultrafundamentalists and the far right unanimously endorse the statement, "Let's get the United Nations out of the United States and the United States out of the United Nations." During the mid-1940's McIntire had written, "We have favored the United Nations Organization with the earnest hope that something could be done to help preserve peace with liberty." In 1964, however, he had apparently forgotten his earlier approval when he wrote:

I do believe the United Nations was conceived in sin. Sin is the transgression of the law of God, as we find in the Holy Scriptures. The United Nations virtually made a pact with the Devil when it included the godless Communists and gave them representation in all areas of the new world organization.[9]

The same alarm is sounded for America against every United Nations agency; UNICEF and UNESCO are the most frequent examples of the internal conspiracy. Neither is "Christian"; both favor "world order under law" and both donate propaganda to American schools which subverts the ideals of the nation.[10]

The fundamentalists of the far right find the internal conspiracy feverishly working to dominate domestic as well as foreign policy. The trend of American life since the election of Franklin D. Roosevelt clearly shows how sinful this nation has become. Ameri-

[8] Carl McIntire, *Author of Liberty*, pp. 209-10; see also an article by Lt. Howard E. Parkinson, U.S.N.R., "The Bible—A Guide for War," *Christian Beacon*, May 26, 1955, p. 3.

[9] McIntire, *Author of Liberty*, pp. 195-96; *Christian Beacon*, Dec. 10, 1964, p. 4; Hargis, "This I Believe," pp. 5-7. Another contradiction develops here because the far right has also stated that only Communist bloc nations should be expelled from the United Nations; see note 7 in this chapter for documentation.

[10] See the Twentieth Century Reformation pamphlet, "Cooperation with Communists in UNICEF"; Hargis, *The Weekly Crusader*, Sept. 21, 1962; Walker, *The Christian Fright Peddlers*, p. 241. For a strong defense of UNICEF by a well-known conservative see the address by Dr. Walter Judd in U.S., Congress, House Record, *Congressional Record*, 1962, 108, pt. 12, 16532-34; *Christian Beacon*, June 30, 1955, p. 8.

can leaders have moved away from fidelity to principle; they have betrayed the Founding Fathers to please the masses. Give-aways, federal subsidies, welfare, deficit finance, consensus, bureaucracy, red tape, new taxes, unlimited credit, installment buying, and pay-as-you-go tax collections were but some of the diabolically clever signs of how far America has gone down the road to Moscow and Peking. If a handout is wrong, it is wrong regardless of how many people vote for it. The majority is not often correct. In fact, the real American knows it is usually wrong because it fails to accept self-discipline or restrictions on its insatiable desire for instant satisfaction.

The trouble with Americans has been their readiness, their eagerness to sell out. They vote for the lawmakers who offer the most, regardless of the price. The legislator with backbone would not compromise, he would not seek a consensus. He would see the sham of "pluralistic politics" and vote for righteousness every time.[11]

This is not unreasonable; this is not an insuperable goal. The answers are in the Bible, if only one has the wit to read it correctly. For instance, the Scriptures speak clearly in telling Americans what to do about poverty. The worst thing that could happen is already here, the "War on Poverty." To the ultrafundamentalists that program could not help but fail, since it took away the initiative from those who wanted to help themselves and saddled the successful citizens with the problems of the indolent, the lazy, and the weak. McIntire writes, "the best remedy for poverty is the Word of God." Dr. Hargis suggests "much more could be done for the poor if it was taken out of the hands of the government and left to religious and charitable private organizations as it was in the past."[12]

[11] Two helpful analyses of the response by the far right to modern life, both of which draw heavily on behavioral research findings, are John Bunzel, *Anti-politics in America: Reflections on the Anti-political Temper and its Distortions of the Democratic Process* (New York: Alfred A. Knopf, 1967), chap. 2, and Joseph R. Gusfield, *Symbolic Crusade: Status Politics and the American Temperance Movement* (Urbana: University of Illinois Press, 1963), pp. 140-60; also see *Christian Beacon*, March 18, 1965, p. 2; McIntire, *Author of Liberty*, pp. 168-76; Hargis, *The Weekly Crusader*, June 1, 1962, pp. 1-2 and July 20, 1962, *passim*.

[12] *Christian Beacon*, April 16, 1964, p. 2 (the proof text is Matt. 26:11); the Twentieth Century Reformation pamphlet, "What the Bible Says About

Medicare comes under the same indictment as an enemy of America. In 1962, the ACCC labeled it as "totalitarian" and concluded it "is contrary to the principles of liberty, morality, and individual responsibility" protected by the Ninth and Tenth Commandments. Medicare would give the government control over a person's body; he could no longer make his own decisions. Good Americans know Medicare has been for many years "a prime goal of the international Communist conspiracy." [13]

The ultrafundamentalists hail the American experience as proof that God-fearing people from diverse backgrounds can live together in freedom and peace. However, the ACCC–ICCC leaders have consistently advocated a rigid tightening up of immigration laws. For instance, they find the liberalist-socialist-Communist conspiracy at work in the repeal of the McCarran-Walter immigration law. Their reasoning in this instance was not based directly on Scriptural proof texts. Rather, they stated that the old, national origins system is "America's first line of defense" against undesirable foreign elements. Since liberal and nonseparationist clergymen worked for repeal of McCarran-Walter, that fact in itself proved how the Communists felt about it.

Hargis and McIntire worked through a far right organization, the American Coalition of Patriotic Societies, to maintain the older restrictions on Europeans of Mediterranean and Slavic backgrounds. One of the coalition's publications argued that the abolition of the national origins system would lead to a "conglomeration of racial and ethnic elements" which would produce "a serious cultural decline" in America. Of the forty-six people listed as members of the "Board of Advisors and Endorsers" of Christian Crusade, only one name is of Balkan or Italian origin.[14]

Poverty"; McIntire, *Death of a Church*, chap. 10; *The Weekly Crusader*, April 19, 1963, p. 6.

[13] In the November 25, 1948, issue of *Christian Beacon*, p. 6, McIntire reprints an article by a Pennsylvania doctor (M.D.), identifying himself with the American Medical Association and stating, "We are afraid of socialized medicine because of its communist implications"; see also the May 10, 1962, issue, p. 3; a Hargis pamphlet, "Uncle Sam, M.D.?"; Hargis, "American Socialism . . . Moving America Downhill," p. 9.

[14] See the Coalition pamphlet, "Immigration: Our Open Door Policy" (n.d.), p. 3; it was distributed by Christian Crusade and other groups; Hargis, *Communist America—Must It Be?*, pp. 157-58; see the resolution against repeal in *Christian Crusade*, September, 1964, p. 9. The one exception, Matt Cvetic, is an ex-Communist; Redekop, *The American Far Right*, pp. 97, 160.

The ultrafundamentalists have spoken out on many other domestic issues. They oppose urban renewal, they favor boycotting imported Communist goods. Perhaps their most important demand in domestic affairs is for the repeal of the Sixteenth Amendment, the progressive income tax, in favor of what they and the entire far right call "The Liberty Amendment." No other proposal they have made expresses the full power of their bitterness bordering on hatred for modern America. In one, clean magnificent sweep this nation can do away with welfare programs, deficit finance, relief rolls, high salaries for government officials, and everything else the ultrafundamentalists find objectionable that is financed by tax revenue. Since the government is too bloated and too strong, it can be cut down to size by taking away its money. It is as simple as that.

To replace the income tax, Congress would enact the Liberty Amendment.

Section 1. The Government of the United States shall not engage in any business, professional, commercial, financial or industrial enterprise except as specified in the Constitution.

Section 2. The constitution or laws of any State, or the laws of the United States shall not be subject to the terms of any foreign or domestic agreement which would abrogate this amendment.

Section 3. The activities of the United States government which violate the intent and purposes of this amendment shall, within a period of three years from the date of the ratification of this amendment, be liquidated and the properties and facilities affected shall be sold.

Section 4. Three years after the ratification of this amendment the sixteenth article of amendments to the Constitution of the United States shall stand repealed and hereafter Congress shall not levy taxes on personal income, estates and/or gifts.

This proposal was discussed and rejected by Congress in 1961. At that time its critics pointed out that its enactment would create anarchy in the nation. A brief summary of some of the government services it would abolish will suggest how sweeping its effects would be. The amendment would do away with Social Security and the Veterans Administration, including its hospitals. Other services which would have been abolished include

the Forestry Service, the Federal Housing Authority, the Federal Reserve Banks, the TVA, the Patent Office, the National Labor Relations Board, the National Park Service, the Postal Savings System, the Atomic Energy Commission, the Bureau of Public Roads, the Central Intelligence Agency, the Civil Aeronautics Administration, the Civil Defense Administration, the Soil Conservation Service, the Water Conservation Division, and many other Federal activities.[15]

By the late 1960's, the ultrafundamentalists were still working vigorously for the adoption of this amendment.

The Supreme Court is singled out by the radical right and the ultrafundamentalist for thorough denunciation. In part, this bitterness is due to the fact that the court cannot be controlled or influenced by pressure groups or political parties. Its decisions can overrule bills of Congress and laws of legislatures. Its decisions can be overturned only by the long and difficult process of constitutional amendment. So long as the liberal establishment continues to dominate the court, America will jump to Moscow's tune.

Chief Justice Earl Warren has come under special attack as the personification of all that the ACCC–ICCC leaders find objectionable in the court. Dr. McIntire wrote that both President Lyndon Johnson and The Worker (a Communist paper) suggested Justice Warren be appointed as head of the commission to investigate the assassination of President Kennedy. McIntire's statement produced considerable criticism, and sometime later he explained he

[15] Arnold Forster and Benjamin R. Epstein, Danger on the Right, pp. 167, 169; Redekop, The American Far Right, pp. 76, 108; John Stroman, "The American Council of Christian Churches," Ph.D. diss., Boston University, 1966), pp. 209-10; see McIntire's analysis in two pamphlets, "For Religious Reasons: Abolish the Income Tax," and "The Liberty Amendment"; Christian Beacon, Dec. 17, 1964, p. 8; "Highlights: Christian Crusade Third Annual Anti-Communist Leadership School, 1964," see Resolution no. 3, p. 6.

did not mean to imply that the president or Warren were taking orders from the Communist party. McIntire concluded, "but it was a very significant and interesting coincidence." He did not explain what he meant by "significant." [16]

As to the court decisions, the ultrafundamentalists argue the constitution never granted that body the powers it has used in ruling on desegregation in public schools, in prohibiting religious exercises in public schools, in all dealings with the American Communist Party, and in tightening the procedural processes of governmental investigating agencies, including those of Congress. In their judgment, which is shared by the full radical right, the Supreme Court has reversed the Protestant traditions on which America was founded. Unless its powers are checked, the United States has only "the dark night of slavery and tyranny" ahead.[17]

In the view of the ACCC–ICCC leaders, the trend toward communism which emerges clearly from a study of domestic issues is also obvious throughout American education. On every level of learning, historic Protestantism is being destroyed and free enterprise and republican self-government are being ignored or ridiculed. The schools are dominated by "ideas that the Communists find as useful allies: religious agnosticism, which is called 'higher learning': and anti-Americanism which is called 'academic freedom.'" The Church League of America finds the soft-on-communism liberals using the "magic fire-wall" of academic freedom to spread their subversive ideologies.[18]

The major indictment by the fundamentalists of the far right is found in two books, Verne Kaub's *Communist-Socialist Propaganda in American Schools* and E. Merrill Root's *Brainwashing in the High Schools* (see p. 109). Both authors find the

[16] *Christian Beacon,* Aug. 13, 1964, pp. 1, 8.

[17] Among the many ultrafundamentalist titles on this subject see the Christian Crusade pamphlets, "Six Men Against God" and "The Supreme Court Mess and Our Christian Foundations"; the Twentieth Century Reformation has a packet, "Project America II," with many related items; the Church League of America has a "Special Report: The United States Supreme Court," Jan., 1965; Redekop, *The American Far Right,* pp. 41, 97.

[18] Hargis, "This I Believe," p. 4; *News and Views,* Jan., 1966, p. 4; Hargis believes the principle of academic freedom is a Communist trick; see *The Weekly Crusader,* Dec. 7, 1962, p. 1; in McIntire's judgment the National Educational Association and the Parent-Teachers Association contribute to pro-Communist thinking; see his publication, "The NEA and the PTA."

internal conspirators busy peddling their insidious dope through textbooks to vulnerable young people. Both authors sharply criticize the National Education Association, which they find promoting false ideals. The PTA has also shown a consistent soft-on-communism line.

The far rightists suggest several remedies. Patriots should reinstate the McGuffey Readers of the late nineteenth century. Those texts unashamedly extolled the virtues of Christian America. Today many far right bookstores sell these readers. Second, the *Christian Beacon* pointed out that some "conservative Christian theologians" have called on fellow Christians in local school districts "to be increasingly alert and aware of what is being taught in the public schools, how it is being presented, and what controls can be exercised to insure courses fairly presenting American history and the conservative principles of Constitutional government." [19] Finally, supporters of the ACCC–ICCC viewpoint are urged to send their children to private schools or to Shelton or Highland colleges, or Bob Jones University where the kind of education America needs is being taught.

The Associate Evangelist of Christian Crusade discovered the rock-and-roll music popularized by the Beatles is, in fact, the product of communism and communist front leaders. These anti-Americans know how to use rhythm, beat, and words for indoctrinating the youth of America into believing their lawless doctrines of riot and revolution.[20]

Both Drs. McIntire and Hargis have commented on the fluoridation of water, another issue closely associated with the far right crusade. Dr. McIntire is unconvinced science has proved its case for the decay preventative, and sees the real issue as involving "individual freedom of the citizens and the acceptance of a socialistic concept." He believes a community's officials are acting as socialists when they use public utilities such as water for

[19] *Christian Beacon,* Sept. 10, 1964, p. 2; Raywid, *The Ax-Grinders, passim;* Jack Nelson and Gene Roberts, Jr., *The Censors and the Schools* (Boston: Little, Brown, 1963), chap. 4 and p. 158.

[20] David Noebel, two pamphlets, "Communism, Hypnotism and the Beatles," and "Rhythm, Riots and Revolution"; neither Dr. McIntire nor Mr. Bundy have commented on the Beatles. The Young Americans for Freedom were not impressed with the Noebel argument; see the critical review in their journal, *The New Guard,* June, 1965, p. 18.

what they consider to be programs for improving the community's health. This is "creeping socialism"; those who want fluoride should purchase it at a drugstore. Dr. Hargis finds Communists urging Americans to use fluoride.[21]

A succinct summary of the ultrafundamentalists' viewpoint was made by the California congregations of the American Council of Christian Churches, in 1964, shortly after the national elections. The *Christian Beacon* reported the proceedings. In discussing the "Great Society" they concluded:

Since socialism ultimately involves the substitution of the state for the provision and salvation of an Almighty God, destroys the freedom of the individual and openly repudiates the Bible's message of a crucified and coming Saviour, it must be rejected and resisted by those who love the Word of God.

In fewer words, but with greater pungency, a Christian Crusade leader made his summary. "A special place in hell is being reserved for people who believe in walking down the middle of the political and religious road. It will be their privilege to fry with Eleanor Roosevelt and Adlai Stevenson." [22]

The supreme expression of the ultrafundamentalist's devotion to Christian Americanism is his exposure of the nation's organized church life. There, more than anywhere else, he finds the most corrupting features of the internal conspiracy at work. As a churchman himself, he mobilizes every resource of his theology, ideology, and action program to destroy America's most dan-

[21] A Twentieth Century Reformation tract, "Fluoridation and Individual Liberty"; a news item in *Christian Crusade*, April, 1966, p. 6; an excellent study with a bibliography is John E. Mueller, "The Politics of Fluoridation in Seven California Cities," *The Western Political Quarterly*, March, 1966, pp. 54-67.

[22] *Christian Beacon*, Dec. 17, 1964, p. 3; Pete Martin, "I Call on Billy James Hargis," *Christian Herald*, Feb., 1967, p. 20; Bundy delivered a summation address in Houston in 1961 in which he stated that each of the following were aiding communism in America: "the churches and church leaders, educators, newspapers, the YWCA, the American Civil Liberties Union, the White House advisers for the Peace Corps, the Supreme Court, and thousands of Americans 'who have been duped by the Communist front organizations' . . ."; Willie Morris, "Houston's Superpatriots," *Harper's*, Oct., 1961, p. 50; *News and Views*, Dec., 1967, p. 5.

gerous enemy within—the nonseparated church member. No words are too strong, no amount of money is too large for the war which must be waged against Satan and his lieutenants posing as Christians. Knowing he is freed from the judgment of God, with the full assurance that whatever he says is absolutely correct, the fundamentalist of the far right achieves his moment of fulfillment when he convinces an individual, a group, or a congregation to separate totally from the apostate establishment and walk into the pure air of the American and International Councils of Christian Churches.

At this point a question must be raised: Has the ultrafundamentalist made any appreciable inroads into the mainstream of American church life? Since its principle task is to lead a twentieth-century reformation, has it succeeded? The balance of this chapter is devoted to a circuitous answer to those questions. No direct, unequivocal answer can be made because, to the best of my knowledge, no one has produced conclusive data or statistics showing how many specific congregations or individuals have separated due to the express influence of the ACCC–ICCC. Separations have occurred, to be sure. The *Christian Beacon, Christian Crusade,* and Church League publications such as "The Record of the NCC" quickly publish accounts of any such division. However, no one has proven conclusively that the motivation for separation, in more than widely isolated cases, was created by McIntire, Hargis, Bundy, or Kaub. Congregations have divided for many reasons; speaking in tongues, financial discord, personalities, civil rights activism, or liturgical innovation. None of these were necessarily the direct response to ultrafundamentalist proselytizing.

Leaving motivation out of the picture, one might conclude that some reliable statistical data are available which show at least some kind of trend. Unfortunately, this information does not exist. The major Protestant churches publish their membership statistics annually in the *Yearbook of American Churches,* but obviously have no explanations as to why particular individuals or portions of congregations leave the denomination. It is altogether possible the major bodies are not anxious to publicize any separation based on ultrafundamentalist leadership.

The ACCC–ICCC denominations do not contribute much

156

help with the statistical record. Since the *Yearbook* is compiled and published by the National Council of Churches, and since the ACCC–ICCC believe any contact with that council is evil, they refuse to send it their membership figures. It is possible that when a separation occurs, as reported in the *Christian Beacon*, the ultra-fundamentalists give it maximum publicity and read their own conclusions into the motives of those separating.[23]

One thorough study has been made of this problem. Dr. John Stroman, a Methodist clergyman, wrote his doctoral dissertation at Boston University on "The American Council of Christian Churches." After presenting his evidence he concluded: "There is not a single denomination that has withdrawn from the National Council as a direct result of the American Council." [24] Neither he nor anyone else has been able to make an exhaustive, quantitative study of ultrafundamentalist influence on the local level of church life. Undoubtedly, individuals have withheld funds to the local church and sent them to ACCC–ICCC offices. Undoubtedly individuals, inspired by ultrafundamentalist leaders, have been influential in the selection or withdrawal of books in public and church libraries, and in electing individuals to church council offices and related activities. However, in a nation as large as the United States, it is futile to think that any adequate, comprehensive analysis of local influence can be made.

What can be explored with some certainty is, first, the nature of the ultrafundamentalist's criticism of organized church life and, second, the manner in which this offensive is conducted. The guiding principle, so deeply revered by every ultrafundamentalist is taken from Jude 3:

> Beloved, when I gave all diligence to write unto you of the common salvation, it was needful for me to write unto you, and exhort you that ye should earnestly contend for the faith which was once delivered unto the saints.

Placing themselves in the company of the saints, the fundamentalists of the far right speak out in a manner and with a

[23] For further elaboration on the difficulty of obtaining reliable membership data see Gasper, *The Fundamentalist Movement*, chap. 2.
[24] Stroman, "The American Council of Christian Churches," p. 269; his discussion of statistics is presented on pp. 106-32.

vocabulary completely distinct in American church circles. They deny that the harshness of their language and the self-assurance of their judgments are out of harmony with the Christian virtues of modesty, humility, and respect for others. One spokesman wrote, "Let us reply only that we are not in the business of attacking other Christians." [25] This sounds laudable but it is actually misleading because ultrafundamentalists consider only those in complete harmony with them to be Christian. Hence, they consider all nonseparationists fair game for verbal assault.

The most adequate means of portraying the nature and style of the ACCC–ICCC indictment of the churches is to present a series of its indictments. The reader can judge for himself whether these are "attacking other Christians."

In commenting on an article from "The Lutheran Hour News" of the Rev. Oswald Hoffman, sponsored by the Lutheran Church–Missouri Synod, the *Christian Beacon* stated:

An article such as is here presented could never have been written by a man [Hoffman] who was forthright in his handling of Biblical truth in opposing Communism. . . . The Lutheran Hour has gone "soft" and if the view which it is presenting here of a positive opposition is accepted by the Lutherans generally, they will have departed from the spirit and militancy that was characteristic of Martin Luther in dealing with error.[26]

In commenting on a statement made by a former president of Union Theological Seminary, New York, a *Christian Beacon* writer stated, "I saw the Devil in that man. I felt him. The conflict in which we are now engaged has the deepest spiritual reality." [27] In discussing a well-kown church journal, Dr. McIntire wrote: *"The Lutheran,* published in Philadelphia and serving the United Lutheran Church, appears to be doing what it can to destroy the Christian religion." [28] In another statement the *Christian*

[25] *Christian Beacon,* Oct. 1, 1964, p. 2; see McIntire's longer study, *The Epistle of the Apostasy: The Book of Jude* (Collingswood, N. J.: Christian Beacon Press, 1959).
[26] *Christian Beacon,* Jan. 11, 1962, p. 3.
[27] *Ibid.,* Jan. 25, 1962, p. 2.
[28] *Ibid.,* March 9, 1961, p. 4.

Beacon declared that the journal entitled *The Episcopalian* was destroying the missionary program and "everything that could be called Christian." [29]

The ultrafundamentalist indictment is not restricted to churches supporting the Protestant ecumenical movement. Many other well-known church groups and periodicals often receive the same kind of criticism. Among these are the Moody Bible Institute, *The Sunday School Times,* Calvin College, *The Reformed Journal,* Fuller Theological Seminary, Youth for Christ, Inter-Varsity Christian Fellowship, the American Bible Society, and Dr. Carl F. H. Henry, editor of *Christianity Today.* The new evangelicals, made up primarily of members of the National Association of Evangelicals are, in McIntire's judgment, "more abusive and do more harm to the cause of the Gospel and the purity of the Church than the liberals themselves." Even the fundamentalist, Dr. Theodore Epp, and his "Back to the Bible" radio program are rejected as being non-Christian.[30]

Just as they suspect the United Nations as the harbinger of a "world government," the ultrafundamentalists find every ecumenical movement outside their ranks as proof of the growing "world church" foretold in the Book of Revelation. Every interdenominational body belongs to this movement, be it the National Association of Evangelicals, the National Council of Churches, the Consultation on Church Union, the Roman Catholic Church, the mergers of smaller denominations, or the World Council of Churches.

Dr. McIntire finds in premillennialism the explanation for ecumenicism. The true believer sees the strategy used to build the grand alliance: Rome, Moscow, and the World Council of Churches are steadily moving toward the day as one organic body they will rule the world.

[29] *Ibid.,* Oct. 5, 1961, p. 1.
[30] *Ibid.,* Nov. 3, 1966, p. 1; Hargis has not criticized the groups or individuals referred to in this paragraph. The ultrafundamentalist comments on Moody are in the July 23, 1964, issue, p. 3; on the *Sunday School Times,* Nov. 12, 1964, p. 5; on Calvin College and *The Reformed Journal,* March 25, 1965, *passim;* on the American Bible Society, April 16, 1964, p. 4 and Dec. 14, 1967, p. 2; on Fuller, July 15, 1965, p. 6, where it is stated Fuller people "Preach compromise with Hell"; on Dr. Henry, May 3, 1962, p. 3; on the IVCF and YFC, see Carl McIntire, "Testimony of Separation," p. 84; on Epp, see McIntire, *Outside the Gate,* chap. 16.

Truly, as Revelation says, it is "become the habitation of devils, and the hold of every foul spirit, and a cage of every unclean and hateful bird." This is the apostate, inclusivist church.

Revelation also says that this great whore committed fornication with the inhabitants of the earth and with the kings of the earth. Rome has been doing it for years; the World Council of Churches is beginning to do it.[31]

As devoted as they are to their standards of purity, the fundamentalists of the far right concede that some individuals still remaining within apostate denominations have temporarily been able to hold fast to pure doctrine and Christian Americanism. The ultrafundamentalists have adopted a policy of temporary coexistence with those supporters who someday may find the courage to leave "the unclean thing" by separation. This section will illustrate the nature and style of ACCC–ICCC influence within several major church bodies.

The Protestant Episcopal Church has come under attack from clergymen and lay groups who work closely with the far right. The best known of these, perhaps, is the Rev. T. Robert Ingram, Rector of St. Thomas School in Houston, Texas. He contributes articles and lectures to Christian Crusade. He is a strong opponent of present-day ecumenicism and has edited a series of essays highly critical of racial desegregation.[32]

Another Episcopalian clergyman, the Rev. James P. Dees, did accept and adopt the ultrafundamentalist indictment of American church life. He formally renounced his ordination vows and founded a new body called "The Anglican Orthodox Church." Dees carefully identified it with the Twentieth Century Reformation and the ICCC. His basic complaint, notably political, was the high degree of the "International Communist conspiracy" which

[31] Carl McIntire, *Modern Tower of Babel*, p. 132.
[32] Ingram's theology does not embrace total separation; see *Christian Crusade*, Jan., 1964, pp. 16-17; James Graham Cook, *The Segregationists* (New York: Appleton-Century, 1962), pp. 218-22. Another disenchanted Episcopalian clergyman is the Rev. Paul H. Kratzig who privately published "The NCC and the Social Revolution" (Victoria, Texas, 1965).

he found being promoted within the framework of the Episcopal Church." [33]

Several of the many Baptist groups in the United States have been active in promoting ACCC–ICCC programs. Perhaps the best known is that of the late Rev. Harvey Springer, pastor of the First Baptist Church, Englewood, Colorado. He edited a weekly paper, *Western Voice,* which contained the standard ultrafundamentalist criticism of American life. He also reprinted articles of Dr. Hargis. Of special interest was Springer's concern over Roman Catholic domination of American society. His paper advertised such studies of that subject as *Convent Life Unveiled,* and he actively campaigned against the nomination and election of Senator John F. Kennedy for the presidency.[34]

The style of ultrafundamentalist influence is seen in the work of two Baptist institutions, the San Francisco Conservative Baptist Theological Seminary and the Indiana Fellowship of Regular Baptist Churches. Both publish regular house organs with articles by ACCC–ICCC leaders; both recommend the purchase of books and pamphlets by those spokesmen, and both offer a variety of these titles for sale. These papers help spread the ultrafundamentalist criticisms to church members who otherwise might lack the resources or the knowledge needed for their procurement.[35]

Among Roman Catholics, the publications of two far right

[33] *Christian Beacon,* April 2, 1964, p. 2; April 16, 1964, p. 5; the quotation is from his printed "Statement" on reasons for withdrawing, available from the Committee of Christian Laymen (Woodland Hills, California); Group Research, Inc. *Report,* Sept. 27, 1965, p. 15 cites a *St. Louis Post-Dispatch* story stating Dees had by that date organized twenty-one congregations in fifteen states as well as being an editorial advisor to the Citizen's Councils and an official of Liberty Lobby; see also a critical view by the Rev. Lester Kinsolving, "The Coup That Impends: Episcopalian Extremism," *The Nation,* Jan. 23, 1967, pp 105-8.

[34] See the *Denver Post* for these issues: April 25, 1960; Sept. 18, 1960; Oct. 18, 1960; Nov. 15, 1960; Berton Dulce and Edward J. Richter, *Religion and the Presidency: A Recurring American Problem* (New York: The Macmillan Co., 1962), pp. 198-99; *Western Voice,* May 6, 1965, p. 2; April 25, 1963, p. 1; Feb. 18, 1965, *passim; New York Times,* Sept. 17, 1960, p. 14 and Oct. 16, 1960, pp. 1, 56.

[35] See the Seminary's pamphlet, "Has Communist Thought Penetrated the Church?"; it should be made clear not all Conservative Baptist Associations adhere to this viewpoint; see also the seminary's paper, *The Blu-Print* for March 10, 1964, and May 5, 1964; *Christian Beacon,* Dec. 10, 1964, p. 6; May 13, 1965, p. 1; Nov. 4, 1965, p. 7; and Sept. 9, 1965, p. 8.

action programs suggest that their editors draw heavily from ultra-fundamentalist publications. The Cardinal Mindzenty Foundation of St. Louis, Missouri, and the weekly newspaper, *The Wanderer* of St. Paul, Minnesota, publish items which closely harmonize with those of McIntire, Hargis, and Bundy.[36] These two groups also recommend the writings of Bundy and John Stormer.

The Methodist Church has been criticized by a variety of groups who remain within its ranks, but who accept the indictment of the fundamentalists of the far right. Two small but active laymen's groups reflecting this influence are the Methodist Laymen of North Hollywood, and the United Society of Methodist Laymen of Texas. As do the other groups listed above, they circulate frequent newsletters and promote far right literature to their members.[37]

The same mode of operation is carried out by several groups within Lutheranism. Some members responded very favorably to McIntire's charge that the leadership of the Lutheran World Federation reflected creeping apostasy. He found "the inclusivist pro-Communist line" in Lutheran seminaries, colleges, and Sunday school publications. The growing unity among Lutherans, he charged, was one more sign the "one-world church" and "one-world government" were taking over the nation.

These and similar charges have been given wide circulation in two independent newspapers published by Lutheran clergymen, *Through to Victory* and *Lutheran News* (renamed *Christian News* in 1968). Both editors concentrate on the targets most popular with the ACCC–ICCC: the United Nations, the Supreme Court, Martin Luther King, Bishop James Pike, the National Council of Churches, and the like. Both print articles highly laudatory of Bundy, Hargis, and McIntire. The editor of the *Lutheran News*

[36] The Mindzenty group is headed by three Schlaflys: Miss Eleanor, Mrs. Phyllis (author of *A Choice, Not an Echo*) and her husband, Mr. Fred John Schlafly. One Catholic editor-priest believes that in southern New Jersey, McIntire's attacks have led some Catholics to join the John Birch Society; S. J. Adamo, "Catholics and the John Birch Society," *Jubilee*, July, 1966; more details on Catholic problems with the far right are in A. V. Krebs, Jr., "A Church of Silence," *Commonweal*, July 10, 1964, pp. 467-76.

[37] *Christian Beacon*, Jan. 14, 1965, p. 4; Oct. 22, 1964, pp. 4-5; and Sept. 2, 1965, pp. 1, 8; the North Hollywood group is endorsed by the Committee of Christian Laymen (see p. 163) in its Publication no. 1, rev. ed. April 1, 1962.

presented a series of lectures on the Christian Crusade radio broadcast.[38]

The effects of these promotions on Lutherans, as with other church members, cannot be measured. The president of the Lutheran Church–Missouri Synod stated that the *Christian News* has had "a very disunifying effect on our church." The majority of one Lutheran Church in America congregation in South Carolina separated from the parent church "due to the effects of Carl McIntire's propaganda on the members of that church." The parishioners obtained the services of a retired Baptist minister who, with the members, viewed the "separation of the races as equal to the Augsburg Confession." [39]

Not all nonseparationists who support the leading ultra-fundamentalists have been satisfied to work within their own denominations. Since the late 1950's, dozens of small laymen's associations totally independent of any ecclesiastical control have appeared across the nation. They carefully submerged the doctrinal differences among their members and placed their heaviest emphasis on promoting the ideology of the far right and McIntire, Hargis, Bundy, and Kaub.

The best known of these by the late 1960's were the Committee of Christian Laymen of California and the National Committee of Christian Laymen of Arizona. While their influence cannot be accurately gauged, they undoubtedly helped promote the programs of the ACCC–ICCC by recommending and selling

[38] *Christian Beacon*, Aug. 22, 1957, pp. 2-3 and Sept. 5, 1957, p. 5; J. B. Matthews produced for the Church League of America a list, "Certain Activities and Affiliations of 181 Lutheran Clergymen" (1963); see also the League's four-issue series, under anonymous authorship, in *News and Views*, Jan., Feb., June, 1961, and May, 1962, entitled "What Is Troubling the Lutherans?"; *Through to Victory*, Nov., 1965, p. 3; July-Aug., 1965, p. 12; and June, 1965, p. 10; *Christian Crusade*, Dec., 1964, p. 24; Hargis wrote Neipp he had heard "many good things" about a Neipp pamphlet; *Through to Victory*, Sept., 1964, p. 7. One of the items sold by *Through to Victory* was an illustrated pamphlet on the civil war in Angola. The editor wrote: "Get this horrible, shocking, sickening book which shows what happened on March 15, when Red-terrorists in one day mutilated and butchered off 200 whites and 300 Negroes and mulattos in peaceful Angola. Contains 18 pages of actual photographs of the atrocities; Jan., 1963, p. 2.

[39] A statement by Pres. Jacob A. O. Preus, quoted in the *Minneapolis Star*, July 15, 1969, p. 10C; John C. Cooper, "Ultra-Conservatives and Lutherans Today," *Lutheran Quarterly* XVIII (Aug., 1966), 221.

books and pamphlets by the four major spokesmen for ultra-fundamentalism.[40]

Still another area in which the nature and style of ACCC–ICCC activity can be found is that of radio broadcasting. Since about 1960, several radio preachers have attempted to present their own interpretations of the internal conspiracy. Few of these succeeded, primarily because they lacked the resources and the talents of the leading fundamentalists of the far right. For instance, I kept records of the many radio evangelists who started their programs on the radio station in Minneapolis-St. Paul which specialized in that kind of programming. The pattern soon became clear; most would last only a few weeks, some a few months, but over this past decade only the McIntire and Hargis broadcasts managed to continue without interruption.

At least three radio orators favorably disposed to ultrafundamentalism were able to attract enough regional support to sustain them for several years. Among these were Dr. C. W. Burpo of Mesa, Arizona. He found contributions coming into his enterprise when he presented the standard far right position on the United Nations, the ecumenical movement, civil rights, "Reds" in the churches, and religious exercises in public schools. By September, 1966, he was broadcasting daily over twenty-six stations in fourteen states.[41]

Another broadcaster who did not reach the top echelons, but who disseminated many ultrafundamentalist ideas on a regional basis during the 1960's, was the Rev. Bill Beeny. He became especially popular after he took up the far right criticism of the civil rights movement. His radio program in 1966 was heard on twenty-six stations. He spoke at rallies at ACCC–ICCC churches where he displayed his "CROSS" home defense unit: Counter Revolutionary Organization on Salvation and Service. This consisted of sawed-off shotguns, revolvers loaded with hollow-point bullets, and a fire-extinguisher device ejecting a chemical with temporary blinding properties. He suggested that this kit was the

---

[40] Both publish regular newsletters which contain these endorsements; both also carry free advertising for privately printed criticisms of American church life.

[41] Group Research *Report,* Sept. 15, 1966; see Burpo's booklet "Sunshine and Shadows" (1966, rev. ed.) and his regular publication, *Bible Institute News,* Sept., 1966, p. 8.

best protection against those crying "Get Whitey." In his Christmas issue for 1966, he suggested that his gift-boxed "Self-Protection Tear-Gas Gun," selling for ten dollars, could be given "to a loved one for their protection." [42] McIntire, Hargis, Bundy, and Kaub, however, have never offered any firearms or related items for sale or suggested their use.

A third regional broadcaster within the ultrafundamentalist camp during the 1960's was Richard Cotton of Bakersfield, California, and his program *Conservative Viewpoint*. In 1965 it was heard over twenty-two stations. Cotton spoke at Christian Crusade meetings and used and recommended the *Christian Beacon, The Wanderer, Christian Crusade, American Opinion,* and other far right publications.[43]

Through their proselytizing, through nonseparated supporters in the major denominations, through laymen's associations and sympathetic radio broadcasters, the fundamentalists of the far right fulfilled their appointed task of earnest contending. Convinced that America's only hope for survival was through a cleansing of the apostates from the churches, they came to be recognized by the full radical right as the leaders in the church-related phase of the crusade to destroy the liberal establishment. They called their programs a Twentieth Century Reformation or a Christian Crusade, identifying themselves with the Luthers and Calvins, persecuted and hated, yet steadily restoring the pure Gospel to the people.

From every verifiable source, however, their infuence fell far short of their own estimates. Indeed, in 1968, a nasty internal dispute over funds and tactics showed how deep tensions ran within the group itself. Membership in the American Council of Christian Churches made no appreciable gains during the 1960's. Contributions to all ultrafundamentalist programs after 1964 fell far short proportionately of the rapid gains made before that year.

[42] *St. Louis Post-Dispatch,* June 27, 1966, pp. 1, 4, and for these issues: April 9, 1961; April 12, 1961; April 23, 1961. The Bible Presbyterian Church of the ACCC in Minneapolis sponsored Beeny as a lecturer; Minneapolis *Star,* Oct. 8, 1966, p. 11A; Beeny's journal is entitled *The Herald of CROSS;* see the December, 1966 issue, p. 7 for the gift suggestion.

[43] *Christian Crusade,* Oct., 1964, p. 12; see Cotton's publication, *Conservative Viewpoint,* especially the April, 1965 "Supplement" and "Richard Cotton's Recommended Reading List."

No appreciable changes could be found in the programs of those they attacked the most vigorously; Billy Graham, the American Bible Society, the National and World Councils of Churches, the National Association of Evangelicals, the major and most of the smaller denominations continued to pursue their own goals without apparent deference to their far right critics. Indeed a good argument can be made that the opposite trend was more the case; in the later 1960's, the churches were showing more social outreach, more involvement in civil rights, more interest in ecumenicity, and more harmony between Catholic and Protestant than ever before.

These developments should not be interpreted as meaning that fundamentalism of the far right has lost any of its considerable power achieved by 1964. Its program has been responsive to the rapid changes in the world; its leaders have been able to shelve one program quickly in favor of another when a change was demanded. Its flexibility undoubtedly led to the loss of some contributors but attracted new ones at the same time. Thus, the sources of its support shifted, but the total number of followers and its total revenue remained reasonably constant. For this reason, I believe that the politics of doomsday will be active on the American scene for the foreseeable future.

8
The Politics Of Doomsday

This chapter is a summary of those features of the movement which are worthy of commendation and those which are unsatisfactory. To forestall the possible criticism that my assessments are too heavily academic and lacking in specific application, I will toward the end present two sets of action programs suggesting what Americans can do to turn back communism. One is written by Dr. Hargis and the other by an official of the Federal Bureau of Investigation. The reader will have the opportunity to judge which of these seems the more adequate within the framework of American traditions.

In summarizing the strengths of ultrafundamentalism, surely one must begin with praise for the policy of its leaders to conduct their programs in an atmosphere open to public scrutiny. Their publications and radio programs are clearly indentified; the materials they distribute are available to anyone on request. It is true some of their supporters do harass and question the integrity of their critics with early morning telephone calls, abusive letters, and unsigned propaganda literature. However, some of the more rabid opponents of this movement are guilty of the same tactics.

In the same spirit, Dr. McIntire frequently reprints in toto the criticisms of his enterprise. On occasion Dr. Hargis has done the same. Their office workers have always replied courteously and promptly to my requests for information.

Some of the critics believe these leaders are motivated primarily by the desire for personal financial profit. It is true the spokesmen do place an enormous emphasis on collections and use aggressive and highly professional fund-raising methods. And since none of these programs publishes a complete, audited annual financial report (such as does Christian Anti-Communism Crusade), the skeptics continue to raise the question of self-interest. However, no evidence exists to show that any of the leaders receives more than a reasonable salary or other remuneration for himself or his staff.

The critics have used the term "neo-Nazis" in discussing the ultrafundamentalists. This charge does not stand up under careful investigation. The critics have undoubtedly confused these men with authentic hate peddlers such as the well-known anti-Semites or Ku Klux Klansmen, where in fact no link exists. I believe the fundamentalists of the far right have created serious confusion and unwarranted mistrust of public and church officials, but they are not neo-Nazis. For instance, they do not call on the government or the mass media to silence their critics.

Their published goals of being "for God and country" and "against Communism" as these stand in print are hardly objectionable. The leaders call on each person to become involved in the many opportunities for public service, and to study carefully the workings of the government on every level. They remind Americans of the treachery, broken promises, and denial of basic freedoms of which communism is guilty. These specific statements reflect the ideals of conscientious citizenship basic to the success of free government.

These meritorious features, however, fail to cancel out the several shortcomings of ultrafundamentalism. These are presented below in no particular order of importance.

In the realm of authoritative judgments, the ACCC–ICCC leaders frequently quote J. Edgar Hoover. However, they do not publish all of the pertinent statements on anticommunism by the director of the F. B. I. Some of these are presented here and are self-explanatory (see also p. 17).

> Over the years, as could be expected, churches and religious organizations have been—and will so remain—targets for communist infiltration. In the past, some clergymen, unfortunately, have been drawn into the communist movement. *But the overwhelming majority of our clergymen are today wholly loyal to our nation and are working valiantly to protect our freedoms. This is not the time for name calling, for unfounded accusations or publicity-seeking charges designed to confuse, divide and weaken.* The clergy of America need the full support of patriotic Americans in our common struggle against the enemy.[1]

In testifying before the Judiciary Committee of the United States Senate, in 1961, Mr. Hoover said:

> Because communism thrives on turmoil, the party is continuously attempting to exploit all grievances— real or imagined—for its own tactical purposes. It is, therefore, almost inevitable that, on many issues, the party line will coincide with the position of many non-Communists. The danger of indiscriminately alleging that someone is a Communist merely because his views on a particular issue happen to parallel the official party line is obvious. The confusion which is thereby

[1] *Crusader*, June, 1961, p. 15, published by the American Baptist Convention; see also his article, "Let's Fight Communism Sanely," *Christian Herald*, Jan., 1962, p. 62. In 1961 the assistant director of the F.B.I. stated to a Methodist meeting:

> To recapitulate, it can be stated factually and without equivocation that any allegation is false which holds that there has been and is, on a national scale, an extensive or substantial communist infiltration of the American clergy, in particular the Protestant clergy. This statement applies with equal force to the Methodists as it does to other religious denominations.

William C. Sullivan, "Communism and Religion in the United States," a mimeographed copy of an address which I obtained on request from the F.B.I. For a discussion on how the ultrafundamentalists attempted to minimize the Sullivan statement see Harry and Bonaro Overstreet, *The Strange Tactics of Extremism*, pp. 274-80.

created helps the Communists by diffusing the forces of their opponents.[2]

In 1964 he stated:

> Let me emphasize that the American civil rights movement is not, and has never been, dominated by the Communists— because the overwhelming majority of civil rights leaders in this country, both Negro and white, have recognized and rejected communism as a menace to the freedoms of all.
>
> But there are notable exceptions—dangerous opportunists and morally corrupt charlatans who would form an alliance with any organization . . . to advance their own power and prestige.
>
> Self-service individuals such as these are not a genuine part of the civil rights movements. Nor are the brick-throwing rabble, nor the raucous hoodlums who have attacked the forces of law and order and have turned orderly protests into nightmares of violence and bloodshed.[3]

To substantiate further their indictment of the liberal establishment, the fundamentalists of the far right enlist the advice and knowledge of several nontheologically trained individuals. Most of these are retired generals or admirals, former F. B. I. employees, or confessed ex-Communists. The supporters of the ACCC–ICCC programs are told these men are "experts." The follower is assured these experts understand Communist strategy better than do almost all of the national security officials in Washington, D. C. What the ultrafundamentalists overlook is the fact that these men, who are devoted and respected citizens, no longer have access to classified or secret information regarding communism. Their previous experience in counterespionage or counterintelligence does not necessarily qualify them as experts on today's issues. The Communists, who are very clever according to the far right, would not act in a pattern that could be detected by these former officials. The Communists know who these men are

[2] J. Edgar Hoover, "The Communist Party Line," U.S., Congress, Senate, Committee on the Judiciary, 87th Cong., 1st sess., Sept. 23, 1961, p. 6.
[3] Minneapolis *Tribune,* Dec. 13, 1964, p. 18A.

and they know these men did understand their earlier strategy. Hence, if the Communists are as bright as the radical right believes, it is reasonable to assume they will change their strategy so the former experts will no longer be able to understand what they are currently doing.

In another realm, the ACCC–ICCC leaders claim their growing number of supporters proves they are making progress with their crusades. However, they flatly refuse to publish any detailed membership lists of their denominations. A tract published in 1965, "The American Council of Christian Churches," gives the general constituent membership figure as 254,070, but provides no further breakdown on that total. To cite another example, McIntire frequently tells his listeners how rapidly the International Council of Christian Churches is growing. Yet, when I wrote ICCC headquarters requesting membership information on the ICCC body to which Hargis belongs, the International Conference of Calvary Tabernacles, the Secretary replied to me, "I am not sure that they are in existence now." [4] One wonders why the ICCC lacks even the most elementary knowledge of its members.

The Twentieth Century Reformation movement proudly identifies itself as the only direct heir of the Protestant Reformation of the sixteenth century. Its spokesmen state that just as Luther and Calvin upheld *Sola Scriptura* against the apostasy of the Roman Catholic Church, so too they uphold the fundamentals against the corrupted churches of today. They equate their earnest contending with the tradition of dissent promulgated by the early reformers. Just as those courageous men suffered the abuse and persecution of the established clergy, so the spokesmen for the American and International Councils feel they too are being persecuted by the Whore of Babylon. [5]

The identification of the ultrafundamentalists with Luther and Calvin has been severely criticized by students of the early Reformation. In recent years, scholars have demonstrated that neither Luther nor Calvin believed in the efficacy of propositional doctrine as defined by the ultrafundamentalists. [6]

[4] R. F. Hamilton to Erling Jorstad, June 17, 1965; see pp. 71-73 for documentation of Hargis' membership in the ICCC.
[5] McIntire, on KUXL, Minneapolis, Jan. 12, 1966.
[6] Roland H. Bainton, "The Bible in the Reformation," in *Cambridge History of the Bible* vol. 1, ed. S. L. Greenslade, (Cambridge: The University Press,

171

Other churchmen have made extensive criticism of the methods used by the ACCC–ICCC to interpret the Bible. One New Testament scholar questions "very much whether it is right for us to propound and defend notions about the mechanics of inspiration. To do so is to transpose the Bible, however unintentionally, from the area of faith to the area of reason, and in this respect to place it under man instead of under God." [7] Another writes that a common error in Bible study "is the treating of single sentences, or even parts of sentences, as if they were all intended as theological propositions, to be used as building blocks in a system." Those who follow that practice quote single verses out of context while dismissing contrary passages and "condemning all who differ with their interpretations as 'doubting God's word.' " [8] A pastor writes, "We are Bible worshippers when we comb the Bible to find evidence for what we believe." He suggests that Christians are worshipping Scripture rather than God when they use it to keep their spouse or their children in check, or to prove that one of the two major political parties is better than the other, or "to prove that America is right and other nations wrong," or that either peace or war is wrong.[9]

This issue merges into a larger question, that of the ultra-fundamentalists' sublime belief that unquestioning loyalty to formal propositional doctrine, as expressed in written creeds, is the only sure measure of a believer's loyalty to Christ. While

---

1963), pp. 1-37; H. H. Rowley, "Authority and Scripture: I," *Christian Century,* March 1, 1961, pp. 263-65; Alan Richardson, "The Rise of Modern Biblical Scholarship and Recent Discussion of the Authority of the Bible," *Cambridge History of the Bible,* pp. 294-338; John T. McNeill, "History of the Interpretation of the Bible," in *The Interpreter's Bible* I, ed. George A. Buttrick et al. (Nashville: Abingdon Press, 1951-57), pp. 115-26; John T. McNeill, *The History and Character of Calvinism* (New York: Oxford University Press, 1954); T. A. Kantonen, *Resurgence of the Gospel* (Philadelphia: Muhlenberg Press, 1948), pp. 129-38; Geddes MacGregor, *A Literary History of the Bible* (Nashville: Abingdon Press, 1968); John S. Setzer, "A Critique of the Fundamentalist Doctrine of the Inerrancy of the Biblical Autographas in Historical, Philosophical, Exegetical and Hermeneutical Perspective" (Ph.D. diss., Duke University, 1964).

[7] Philip Edgecumbe Hughes, "What is the Bible For?," *Christianity Today,* Nov. 19, 1965, p. 184.

[8] L. Harold DeWolf, *The Case for Theology in Liberal Perspective* (Philadelphia: Westminster Press, 1959), p. 49.

[9] Marcus Gravdal, "The Death of Bible Worship," *Lutheran Standard,* Sept. 20, 1966, pp. 3-4.

172

clear definitions are always desirable, the ACCC–ICCC leaders have placed an inordinate amount of confidence in the ability of the human mind to formulate precise knowledge about God and his ways. It will always be an open question as to whether faith is not ineffable, and whether authentic Christian experience is not beyond verbal formulation. Propositional doctrines have a way of emptying out the dimension of mystery inherent in one's own search for such an encounter. The ultrafundamentalists overlook or minimize the enigmas of the supernatural. They consider the miracles of Jesus or the premillennial return as virtual everyday occurrences which do not have to be seen through the eyes of faith, but must be accepted as factual proofs of God's omniscience.

If the fundamentalists of the far right had limited their programs to theological and ecclesiastical matters, the criticisms of their programs could stop at this point. However, they speak out on a wide variety of issues and these are as vital to their cause as doctrine itself.

The fundamentalists of the far right consider themselves to be true political conservatives; they carefully and repeatedly identify themselves with that tradition. While definitions of "conservative" are abundant and varied, one understanding of the term can be reached by taking notice of the voting records and statements of certain nationally prominent lawmakers, such as Senators Karl Mundt or John Tower, or Representative Gerald Ford.[10] None of these legislators have shown interest in those proposals emanating solely from the far right. They have rejected the demand for the immediate withdrawal of the United States from the United Nations, the impeachment of Chief Justice Earl Warren, the abolition of the Sixteenth Amendment in favor of the Liberty Amendment, and the abolition of all foreign aid. If these measures were truly "conservative" one wonders why conservative lawmakers have not endorsed them.

The ultrafundamentalists do very emphatically make their support known for several well-known public officials. A perusal of those names associated with Christian Crusade shows a substantial homogeneity: Ezra Taft Benson, Albert Watson, John R.

[10] One starting point for a definition would be *What Is Conservatism?* ed. Frank S. Meyer (New York: Holt, Rinehart and Winston, 1964), especially pp. 229-32.

173

Rarick, John Rousselot, Bruce Alger, John Bell Williams, and Senator James Eastland.

Both the Twentieth Century Reformation and Christian Crusade give fulsome praise to former Governor George C. Wallace and Senator Strom Thurmond. The enthusiasm for Wallace is especially suggestive concerning ultrafundamentalist conservatism. In 1964, Christian Crusade elected him its "Christian Patriot of the Year." In 1966, McIntire expressed his views after an interview.

> He is a Bible-believing Christian, is fully aware of what the National Council of Churches is seeking to do in the country and to the churches. He reads the *Christian Beacon* regularly. He is not against the Negro; he is for the Negro, desires that they shall have equal rights. The problem which he has fought centers around the question of whether these matters are to be worked out in the States under the Constitution and State's rights or whether it is to be handled in Washington, D. C. under the direction of powerful bureaucratic machinery with the Washington politicians getting credit for it.

McIntire was also impressed with Wallace's own description of his inauguration as governor. No liquor was served and on special request a singer from the Grand Ole Opry in Nashville sang "Please Lord, Put Prayer Back in School." [11]

Perhaps the most conclusive recent evidence showing the strong unanimity existing on candidates and issues between the ultrafundamentalists and the radical right is, first, the roster of speakers at the 1969 Christian Crusade national convention and, second, the support given Dr. McIntire in that year by the best known far right national leaders. At the Crusade meeting the delegates heard as invited speakers: former Governor George Wallace; John Stormer, an official of the ACCC–ICCC; former Major General Edwin A. Walker, and Congressman John Rarick along with the high ranking officials of the Hargis organization. The Wallace address was significant in that it marked the first time any presidential candidate as such had ever addressed a meeting of an

[11] *Christian Beacon,* Jan. 13, 1966, p. 4.

ultrafundamentalist organization. No other candidate for that office has attracted speakers from every wing of the radical right to a national rally.

If any doubt existed over McIntire's political preference and loyalty to radical right leaders, this was erased in the summer of 1969. During a controversy with the New Jersey State Department of Higher Education over the accreditation of Shelton College, McIntire, as president of that college, stated publicly that at the next mass rally in support of Shelton, George Wallace of Alabama would stand beside him "with a Bible in his hand." To underline his support from far right political leaders even more, McIntire, at the rally held to protest the proposed withdrawal of accreditation of Shelton, read letters of support for his cause from Senator Strom Thurmond, Congressman Mendel Rivers, Governor Lester Maddox, and former Governor Wallace. The Alabamian praised McIntire for "the many good works accomplished by you and your institution on behalf of a sound fundamental and patriotic approach to the education of the young. I know also of your efforts to develop and preserve the qualities of character vital to the survival of this nation. For all of this you have and deserve our congratulations and sincere appreciation." [12] What the Crusade convention and the Shelton rally prove is that by 1969, the fundamentalists of the far right were eagerly mixing it up in the political arena, supporting nonseparationists, far more than at any time since the presidential campaign of 1964.

The question arises whether Wallace and his candidacy truly represent the best of contemporary American conservatism as his supporters listed just above claim. In this writer's judgment, the best of that tradition are the Towers and Mundts and Fords; the Russell Kirks, Frank S. Meyers, James J. Kilpatricks, and William F. Buckleys. None of these endorse George Wallace. Nor do any of them show any enthusiasm for the sheltering organization of the far right, the John Birch Society. The record, then, shows the best of American conservatives have not recognized the Wallace phenomenon as representative of their principles.

The real test is whether the ultrafundamentalists themselves really believe their conservatism and specific reform proposals will

[12] *Christian Beacon*, Aug. 7, 1969, p. 2 and July 31, 1969, p. 8.

save America: the Liberty Amendment, no foreign aid, no welfare legislation, no Social Security, no membership in the United Nations, and the rest. The entire radical right believes these phenomena are symptomatic of what they believe to be the tyranny and collectivism of American life brought on by the internal conspiracy. But the ultrafundamentalists are caught up in a profound contradiction at this point, which leaves one unconvinced about their solutions. If righteousness were to triumph in their terms—the Liberty Amendment enacted, Social Security abolished, and so on—this would mean the biblical prophecies were wrong. It would mean the liberal conspiracy had been destroyed and God's elect had gained control of this planet *before* the Pretribulation Rapture and the Battle of Armageddon. But, no fundamentalist of the far right could admit the Bible was wrong in its prophecy or in any way. So this places him in a trap. He advocates a program which if adopted would destroy his most cherished beliefs.

A final question is whether the fundamentalists of the far right offer the most effective program consonant with American traditions for resisting international and domestic communism.

Only history, obviously, will give the final answer. Below are two specific guides for combatting communism. The first is taken from two Christian Crusade pamphlets, "Christian Americans, Unite" and "A Call to Action to Every Real American." (The dots are in the text and do not indicate omissions by me.)

> HERE is what Christian Crusade Chapters DO—Organized monitoring of ultra-liberal broadcasters . . . Enforcement of the Fairness Doctrine . . . Proclaim your support for our men in Viet Nam . . . Challenge the National Council of Churches in your community . . . Combat Liberal news media . . . Militantly oppose liberalism in schools . . . Survey all conservative groups in your area . . . Distribute Christian Crusade and other conservative pamphlets, tracts and books . . . Study constantly, learn and understand the liberal-socialist-communist threat, and discuss it with others . . . Place conservative books in your public library . . . Urge

your support, as an individual, of Christian candidates for public office . . . and PRAY, DAILY.

(1) Join Christian Crusade at once!

(2) Acquire genuine understanding of the communist-socialist menace, so that you can recognize their propaganda, and so that you can speak with authority to your group or in meetings.

(3) Listen to the spendid broadcasts of Dr. Billy James Hargis, Fulton Lewis, Dean Clarence Manion, Dan Smoot, Dr. Carl McIntire, Martha Rountree, Dr. Wayne Poucher and Paul Harvey, and get your family and friends to listen to them.

(4) Distribute pro-American literature to people who are not so well informed as you are.

(5) Make your patriotic views known to office holders, community leaders, and others.

(6) When matters arise requiring united action, get as many people as possible to act.

(7) Get other good Americans to join Christian Crusade as soon as possible.

(Note—We frequently send you material on other things you can do to help preserve America.)

The other set of proposals is made by William C. Sullivan, who at the time they were made was assistant director of the Federal Bureau of Investigation. These were made as part of an address to the Highland Park Methodist Church, Dallas, Texas, October 19, 1961. My copy was sent me by the F.B.I. The specific proposals were reprinted in the *Christian Herald,* January, 1962, p. 63.

1. Start with oneself. Engage regularly in self-examination as a means of better understanding, developing, and applying daily the moral and religious values of our

177

Judeo-Christian heritage. We convince not by words but by example.

2. Study and comprehend fully our nation's social principles, traditions, values, government and historical goals. Relate them correctly to current local, national and international events.

3. Elect government officials who possess intelligence, ability and integrity.

4. Follow systematically the work and decisions of your elected representatives in government and let your views on important issues be known to them.

5. Understand Communist thought, objectives, strategy and tactics.

6. Insist that every citizen is entitled under law to freedom of thought, expression, action, dissent, experimentation, education and worship.

7. Join proven local institutions or establish new organizations designed to improve and strengthen the community. Participate in them regularly and effectively.

8. Eradicate the causes of communism in local communities. These include: poverty, disease, illiteracy, economic dislocation, social injustices, social discrimination, political corruption, education inadequacies, psychological maladjustments, philosophical materialism, religious anemia, and moral decadence—both personal and social.

9. Work steadily toward better relations between races, religions and different social groups and between labor and management.

10. Encourage in one's local community original thinking, intellectual pioneering and moral growth.

11. Contribute to a continuous revitalization of the religious life of the community, beginning with oneself.

12. Stimulate cultural diversity, variety and creativity, for the unity we seek is not uniformity.

13. Help to direct individual and community thinking into constructive action replete with social vision, because it is as true today as it was centuries ago when it was stated that where there is no vision the people perish.

14. Develop and hold forth as a community goal for the young and old alike self-discipline, personal responsibility, dedication to worthy causes, loyalty to basic values and a deep-rooted set of convictions in the inherent dignity and preciousness of every human being and the superiority of a free and open society in which every individual has an equal opportunity to achieve self-realization.

15. Recognize that while there are both permanence and change in life, there is no fixed *status quo;* hence, our need to understand social transitions and to control and to direct these transitions in accordance with the spiritual and moral values of the Judeo-Christian tradition.

The most serious question raised by the ultrafundamentalists is their uncritical identification of their interpretation of Christianity with their understanding of Amercan values and loyal citizenship. Surely all citizens can agree that this nation's ideals are based on Judeo-Christian foundations. That tradition stands as a constant reminder that no individual speaks for God, that no nation is so pure it can dictate the fate of the world, that no nation is immune from the judgment of the eternal God, that no nation can fully embody in its institutions the depth and breadth of God's will for man, and that no nation is ever beyond the need for constant repentance and self-correction.

The Jesus of history and the Christ of faith transcends all of man's efforts to make him into a fundamentalist, a capitalist, or a separationist, or into a conservative, a liberal, or a collectivist. That transcendence points to the God, who, in spite of the imperfections he sees, still loves those he has created.

Index

THE POLITICS OF DOOMSDAY

Internal conspiracy
  and CLA, 75-76
  defined by Christian Crusade, 85-86
  defined by Carl McIntire, 49-50
  defined by Edwin A. Walker, 144-45
  and Democratic Party, 120-21
  and education 78-79
  and Barry Goldwater, 99
  and liberalism, 139-40
  and Joseph McCarthy, 48
  and Supreme Court, 152-53
  ultrafundamentalist view of, 176-77

John Birch Society
  and ACCC, 112
  birth of, 61
  and Edgar C. Bundy, 111-12
  and conservatism, 175
  and finances, 61, 83
  and Barry Goldwater, 99
  and John F. Kennedy, 90-91
  and J. B. Matthews, 109
  and Carl McIntire,, 112-13
  and John Stormer, 108
  and E. L. Wiegand, 111
Jones, E. Stanley, 53-54
"Jesus—A Capitalist," 141

Kamp, Joseph, and Verne Kaub, 77
Kaub, Verne
  biography of, 76-79
  and Carl McIntire, 51
  and Allan A. Zoll, 105
Kennedy, John F., 60
  and Air Force Manual, 83-84

Kennedy, John F.—Cont'd
  assassination of, 89-92
  and Catholic issue in 1960, 66, 118-19
  and civil rights, 92-96
  and communism, 66
  and far right, 82-83
Kennedy, Robert F., 145
Kilpatrick, James J., 175
King, Martin Luther, criticism of, 96, 97
Kirk, Russell, 175
Kuchel, Thomas, 87
Ku Klux Klan, 85, 168
  quote on, by Edwin A. Walker, 108

Larson, Arthur, 76
Liberty Amendment, quoted in full, 151-52, 176
Liberty Lobby, 72
Lory, Milton, 110
Lutheran World Federation, 162
Lutheran, The, 158
Lutheran Church—Missouri Synod, 158, 163
"The Lutheran Hour," 158
Lutheran News. See Christian News
Lutherans and ultrafundamentalists, 162-63

Machen, J. Gresham, 26-33
Maddox, Lester, 175
Matthews, J. B., 109
  and Joseph McCarthy, 48, 55-56
  writes "How Red . . . ?" 51, 78
McCarthy, Joseph R., 46-48
  and Army hearings, 57